FOCUS

'A fascinating and informative look at not only how our attention works, but also how to deploy it more productively and meaningfully in our lives. This is the guidebook you need to master your attention'

Chris Bailey, bestselling author of *The Productivity Project*, *Hyperfocus* and *How to Calm Your Mind*

FOCUS

FUEL YOUR ATTENTION, GET MORE DONE

**MARK TIGCHELAAR
AND OSCAR DE BOS**

SIMON &
SCHUSTER

London · New York · Amsterdam/Antwerp · Sydney/Melbourne · Toronto · New Delhi

First published by Unieboek | Het Spectrum as *Focus AAN/UIT*
First published in English by Simon & Schuster Canada, an imprint of Simon & Schuster, LLC, 2025
First published in Great Britain by Simon & Schuster UK Ltd, 2026
Translated by Vertaalbureau Perfect

Copyright © The Speed Reading Group B.V., 2019

The right of Mark Tigchelaar and Oscar de Bos to be identified as the authors of this work has been asserted in accordance with the Copyright, Designs and Patents Act, 1988.

1 3 5 7 9 10 8 6 4 2

Simon & Schuster UK Ltd
1st Floor
222 Gray's Inn Road
London WC1X 8HB

For more than 100 years, Simon & Schuster has championed authors and the stories they create. By respecting the copyright of an author's intellectual property, you enable Simon & Schuster and the author to continue publishing exceptional books for years to come. We thank you for supporting the author's copyright by purchasing an authorized edition of this book.

No amount of this book may be reproduced or stored in any format, nor may it be uploaded to any website, database, language-learning model, or other repository, retrieval, or artificial intelligence system without express permission. All rights reserved. Inquiries may be directed to Simon & Schuster, 222 Gray's Inn Road, London WC1X 8HB or RightsMailbox@simonandschuster.co.uk

Simon & Schuster strongly believes in freedom of expression and stands against censorship in all its forms. For more information, visit BooksBelong.com.

www.simonandschuster.co.uk
www.simonandschuster.com.au
www.simonandschuster.co.in

Simon & Schuster Australia, Sydney
Simon & Schuster India, New Delhi

The authorised representative in the EEA is Simon & Schuster Netherlands BV, Herculesplein 96, 3584 AA Utrecht, Netherlands. info@simonandschuster.nl

The author and publishers have made all reasonable efforts to contact copyright-holders for permission, and apologise for any omissions or errors in the form of credits given. Corrections may be made to future printings.

A CIP catalogue record for this book is available from the British Library

Trade Paperback ISBN: 978-1-3985-6192-2
eBook ISBN: 978-1-3985-6193-9

Interior design by Ruth Lee-Mui

Printed and Bound in the UK using 100% Renewable Electricity at CPI Group (UK) Ltd

Contents

A Note from the Authors: Busy, but Not Productive — vii

Introduction: Getting a Grip on Focus — 1

PART ONE: TARGETED ATTENTION AND THE FOUR CONCENTRATION LEAKS

Concentration Leak 1: Too Few Stimuli — 14
Focus Challenge: Boredom — 17

Concentration Leak 2: Too Many Internal Stimuli — 34
Focus Challenge: Overscheduling and Overcommitting — 37
Focus Challenge: A Cluttered Mind — 53

Concentration Leak 3: Too Little Fuel — 76
Focus Challenge: Burnout — 79

Concentration Leak 4: Too Many External Stimuli — 102
Focus Challenge: Always Available — 105
Focus Challenge: Too Much Noise — 119

PART TWO: DEEP ATTENTION, CREATIVITY, AND TAKING CONTROL WHEN YOU CAN

The Creativity Paradox: Why Defocusing Is Important for Gaining New Insights	131
Help, My Boss Is Killing My Focus: To What Extent Is Focus a Choice? (Part 1)	143
Addicted to Distractions: To What Extent Is Focus a Choice? (Part 2)	153
Inbox to Zero	163
The End	175
Acknowledgments	177
Glossary	179
Notes	189

A NOTE FROM THE AUTHORS

Busy, but Not Productive

"I get a lot less done these days than I used to, but I'm more tired than ever," my friend Pete says, sighing. We've met up in our favorite bar in Amsterdam and he's sipping his beer with a blank stare.

Pete is one of the smartest people I know. He has a dual degree and was an incredible athlete. Things were always easy for him, but recently he seems to have lost his spark.

"It's incredibly frustrating to be busy all day long, only to find out that you didn't actually get much done at the end of the day," he continues. It's a common complaint we hear in our trainings: busy, but not productive, like you're stuck in first gear.

We often try to solve this issue by speeding up or by planning our time more efficiently, but let's be real: this time management approach is a thing of the past.

Work has become a lot more complex, priorities change all the time, and one important email is all it takes to completely destroy our carefully crafted plans.

This book can help. These days, it's more about focus management: knowing how to shut yourself off from all the stimuli around you, switching between projects more easily, and learning how to actually recharge your brain.

We need it more now than ever before. Since the 1980s, the number of stimuli we're bombarded with every day has quintupled, equal to about 174 newspapers' worth of information daily.[1] We can't really blame ourselves for struggling to focus.

On the one hand, all these stimuli make life thrilling. We're challenged to push ourselves to the limit; it gives us a rush of sorts. But on the other hand, when was the last time you could really dive deep? Read a book without being disturbed? Actually manage to ignore your inbox?

Lots of people have seen their concentration levels drop in recent years, matched by an increase in stress. Working through distractions costs a lot of energy and, worst-case scenario, can leave you burned out.

It shouldn't be like this. You likely chose your job because you wanted to have an impact and make a difference, not to barely survive while playing a constant game of catch-up. Constant work stress isn't right. It's not normal that one in seven people suffers from burnout symptoms.

In this book, we want to show you how you can find your

focus. You'll become more resilient against stress and get more done as a result. It'll even help you when you're not at work: when you're more focused, you're more present during conversations and have more control over your thoughts, which, in turn, makes it easier to relax and fall asleep. Over the course of the book, we'll be working toward calm, clarity, and control.

While writing *Focus On-Off*, we endeavored to apply scientific studies to real-life problems. Our solutions come from recent research in neuropsychology and the experience Oscar and I gained through training and supporting well over one hundred thousand professionals. We have, to the best of our knowledge and abilities, presented scientific research in an understandable way and illustrated how the results can be applied in practice. The results of these studies and the conclusions drawn from them are supported by most scientists, but we realize that some have different opinions. We're always open to discussion and would like to hear about any and all new insights.

We have listed all the references. If we failed to mention anyone who can be shown to have discovered or created a particular line of reasoning or technique, please let us know.

One more thing: To help you decide which themes to tackle first, we've developed a free introductory training course. In a short series of videos, you'll learn how distraction works in your brain and where it often goes wrong. Our AI assistant, Courtney, will ask you a few questions and help you identify your biggest concentration leaks. At the end, you'll receive a personal report with practical tips to regain control. It takes about fifteen minutes. Go to focusacademy.com/introduction.

Let the journey begin!

MARK & OSCAR

PS: Although we created everything together, the book is written in the first person for a smoother read. The "I" in this case refers to Mark.

INTRODUCTION

Getting a Grip on Focus

Before we dive deep, you should know it's not all that strange that we get distracted so easily. From an evolutionary perspective, our brains weren't designed to concentrate on a single task. Just imagine: If you focused fully on peeling nuts in prehistoric times, you might not notice the hungry tiger lurking behind you. Game over. Maybe we should blame natural selection for our inability to focus.* Since it's not very likely that we'll fall victim to a tiger attack at the office, and we've replaced peeling nuts with slightly more complex tasks, shutting ourselves off from all those stimuli has become a useful skill. The question is how?[1]

Some people think the key is to block out the outside world in its entirety, and check your inbox only once a day. This doesn't

---

* This is exactly why we still rear up when someone suddenly taps us on the shoulder while we're fully focused on a task.

seem like a realistic option to me, and it definitely won't make you very popular in the office. Besides, it's not necessary. You don't need to become a hermit or relocate your desk to the middle of nowhere to focus on your work.

A major myth is that concentrating is hard. That's why most people rely on deadlines and caffeine to focus. Although these tools do make it easier to shut yourself off from stimuli, they often come at the price of loads of stress. Stress may be a welcome driver when you're at work, but it can keep your head spinning when you're at home and make it more difficult to fall asleep at night. In the long run, it's just not sustainable.

There's an alternative: understanding how your mind works. In the twenty-one years that Oscar de Bos and I studied this issue, we identified four concentration leaks that cause us to lose focus. In this book, you'll discover exactly what these leaks are and how you can fix them to become more resistant to distraction, get more done, and experience less stress. Before we explain how you can plug these concentration leaks, let's first find out how focus works and what distraction does to our minds.

HOW FOCUS WORKS

All the information that enters our brains through our eyes or ears gets filtered first. And thank goodness for that, because otherwise our thinking brain—the prefrontal cortex—would be completely overwhelmed. Think of the prefrontal cortex as the brain's control room; it's where we analyze information, make decisions, and draw up plans. It's also the part of the brain enabling you to understand these sentences right now. This process used to be called short-term memory, but I've always considered this term somewhat misleading because the prefrontal cortex doesn't really store any information. I prefer calling it our thinking brain.

The part of the brain responsible for filtering information is called the thalamus. The best way to explain how it works is to think of it as your very own personal assistant.

Imagine you're at a party and you're chatting away with people. Suddenly, you hear someone saying your name. Snap! Now that's all you can focus on. Know what I mean? Psychologists have given this phenomenon a very scientific name: the cocktail party effect.

The funny thing is that your name wasn't said any louder than the rest of the conversation. So why did your brain pick up your name, of all things? It's because your brain recorded your neighbor's entire conversation, and your "personal assistant" assessed every word to determine whether it was important enough to let you know. Ultimately, that's why you hear your name, but not the rest of the conversation. Your ears did pick up everything else, but your personal assistant didn't think it was important enough to bother you.

This doesn't just happen with conversations. It happens with every stimulus our senses perceive: someone walking by in a quirky T-shirt, your phone next to you, a passing car, tweeting birds, etc. Every second, eleven million bits of information enter our minds.[2] We're like big walking antennas.

Fortunately, all these stimuli first enter our subconscious minds. If we were aware of every single stimulus our senses perceived, we'd go mad in a split second. To give you an idea of how picky your personal assistant really is: it transmits only

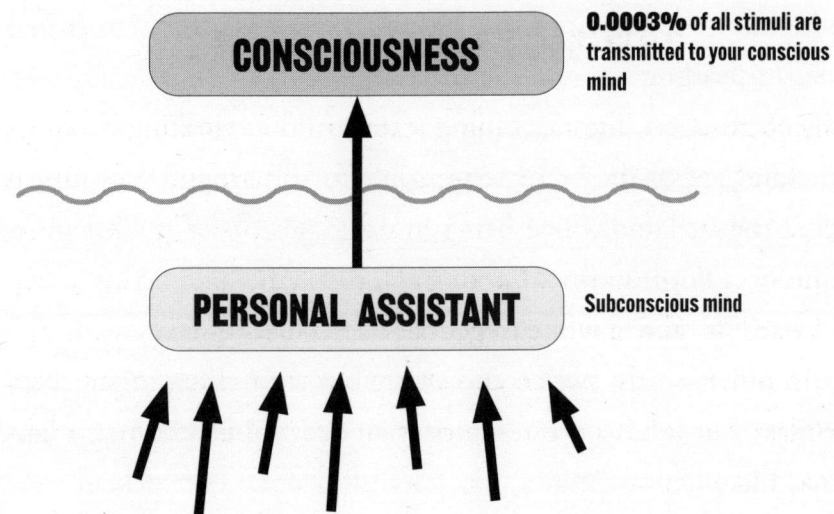

Our minds are constantly bombarded by waves of stimuli. Our personal assistants act as gatekeepers of sorts, carefully selecting which stimuli are transmitted to our conscious minds.

0.0003 percent of the stimuli it perceives to your conscious mind.[3]

And that's focus. It's an incredibly powerful selection tool. It's constantly deciding whether the latest stimulus to reach your mind is more important than whatever you're currently doing. The cocktail party effect isn't restricted to our names. It applies to every piece of information our brains find relevant: information about our hobbies, names of customers, a ringing phone, a car heading straight for us, and so on. If your mind thinks it's important, it'll distract you from whatever you're doing.

This is why lots of people have a hard time focusing in an open space where they're surrounded by coworkers talking about projects they're involved in, but most of us can work easily in a coffee bar packed with complete strangers—same stimuli, but a lot less relevant.

HOW DISTRACTION WORKS

Fully focusing is like reaching a state of flow; working becomes easier and feels as if it requires less effort. You are fully consumed by the task at hand. But getting into the flow usually takes time; we need to boot up first. Getting interrupted is like taking a step backward; it takes a while to get back into the flow.

In other words, switch and you're out. Switching might seem harmless, but it has a greater impact on our brains than you might think. Here's how:

Suppose you're writing a report. It's one of those jobs that you've been putting off, but now you finally made some time for it. A few minutes in, you've found your groove, the words are flowing. Until a colleague drops by: "Do you have a minute?"

Typically, when we make these micro-switches we think about how much time they'll take: What's the harm in answering an easy question? It'll take only a few seconds. The problem isn't how much time switching takes, but how much it affects your brainpower.

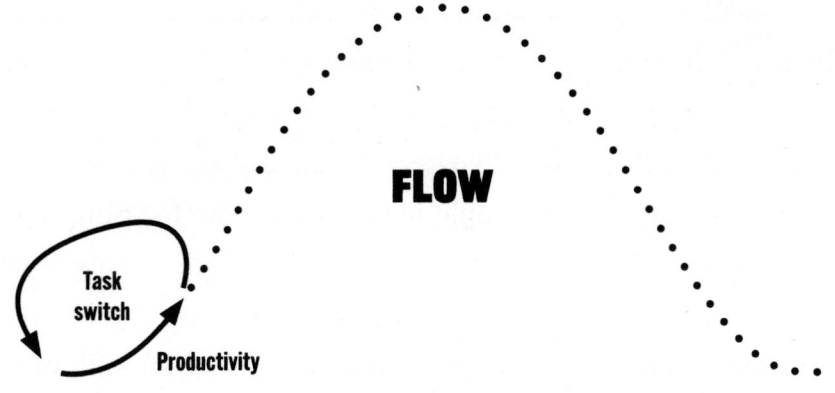

Every time we switch, part of our brains clings to what we were doing before, temporarily lowering our IQ, making it more difficult to continue working. In neuropsychology, we call this *attention residue*: part of our attention lingers with the previous activity, which slows us down and causes us to make more mistakes.[4] This is the main reason concentration leaks are so bad for us.

Practically, here's how it works: When we switch from our own tasks to answering a coworker's question, our brains basically split in two. One part starts crunching out an answer to the question, while the other tries desperately to cling to what we were doing before; we don't want to forget what we were working on! And so our attention is divided.

By the time you resume your original task, the same thing happens again: part of your brain is still caught up in the question, while the other part tries to remember where you left off. This

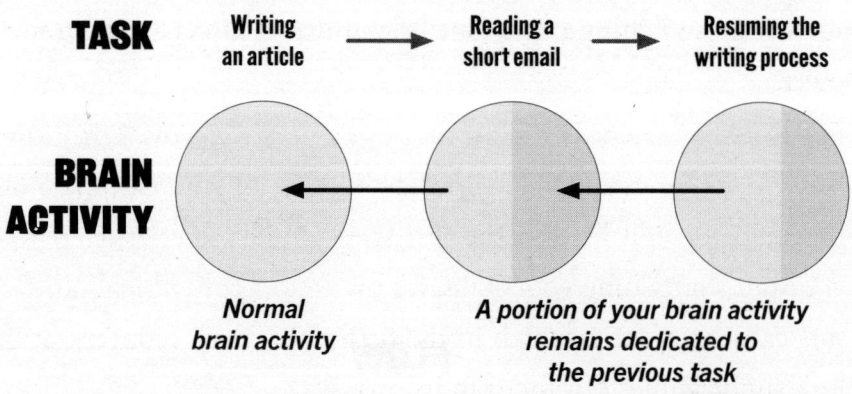

When you hop from one task to another, a portion of your attention will remain dedicated to the previous task, leaving you with less freethinking capacity for your new task.

makes your brain slower and causes you to make about 20 percent more mistakes.[5]

Bizarrely, this phenomenon occurs after even the most subtle attention switches. After a quick peek at your inbox or phone, your IQ temporarily drops by ten points and takes at least a minute to return to normal.[6] If we get sixty emails a day and read each one the second our phone dings, that means we'd spend a full hour a day working with the brain capacity of an eleven-year-old.

When the task we were working on is complex, or if the interruption required a bit more thought, this recovery time can easily skyrocket, costing us fifteen minutes before we're back in a state of flow.[7]

The same applies to hopping from one meeting to another; at each successive meeting, parts of our brains still cling to the previous one, gradually slowing and becoming less sharp. Practical tip: schedule the most complex and important meeting first.

THE FOUR CONCENTRATION LEAKS

Focus management is a game. Your goal is to minimize the number of switches you make in one day. The better you play, the more productive you'll be and the less stress you'll experience. Before you start sharpening your skills, it's useful to know which four factors cause us to task-switch in the first place. Each "concentration leak" undermines our focus in its own way.

Concentration Leak 1: Too Few Stimuli

Our brains are built to optimize. When a task is too slow, too easy, or too boring, they automatically start looking for more stimuli. This makes us efficient, but it's also the main reason our minds wander during conversations, why we find it difficult to focus in noisy offices, why we sometimes reach the end of a page without having any idea what we just read. Once you manage to plug this concentration leak, you'll be better at shutting yourself off from your own distracting thoughts (and the noisy colleagues around you).

Concentration Leak 2: Too Many Internal Stimuli

We tend to blame our phones, emails, and coworkers for our inability to concentrate, but did you know that we're equally effective at distracting ourselves? Fifty percent of the time we lose focus, we have only ourselves to blame.[8] I think we all know the feeling. How many times have you suddenly felt the urge to do something else halfway through a task, then next thing you know you're twenty minutes deep into a social media binge? Or maybe you struggle to fall asleep because every time you start to drift off, your to-do list haunts you, keeping you awake. Our brains are powerful organs, but there's no denying they're exhausting at times. Understanding how this concentration leak works will help you get a grip on it. You'll get better at controlling your thoughts, fall asleep faster, and experience less stress.

Concentration Leak 3: Too Little Fuel

When we're tired, our personal assistants don't function as well. As their ability to determine what is and what isn't important deteriorates, they allow more stimuli to pass through. Effect: if you're tired enough, even the tiniest fly can disrupt your flow. This leak is also the culprit behind productivity dips on those days when you just don't get anything done. Your body might physically be at work, but your mind sure isn't. Once you learn how to recharge your brain properly, this will be much less of a problem.

Concentration Leak 4: Too Many External Stimuli

In other words: our phones, emails, and coworkers. This concentration leak is often the first place we look to improve our focus, but it's the last place we'll find answers. It all begins with getting our minds under control. After that, we can look at how to continue. Only when you're in control—and you'll be well on your way after reading this book—will it make sense to start examining external factors. Don't worry, that's not to say that this book doesn't look carefully at external factors. Later on we'll talk about how to focus in open-plan offices without having to shut yourself off or miss out on anything.

Now, an intriguing question: How often do you think these concentration leaks occur on a daily basis? How often are you interrupted? Don't just count the emails, WhatsApp messages, and coworkers; also count the times when your mind is the culprit. Count all the little moments, like when you remember you need to grab some milk on the way home, dwell too long on an uneasy conversation from the day before, or have a sudden epiphany in the middle of another task. How often do you think this happens over the course of twenty-four hours? I'm curious about your estimate, because, on average, we deal with about five hundred distractions a day. The time we need to recover from all those interruptions means we spend an average of two extra hours at work every day.[9]

Getting a grip on the concentration leaks will help you steady your ship and stop you from switching tasks so often. The goal is to keep you in a state of flow, and make it easier to stay in control as you navigate through the day.

OUR ATTENTION IS SHRINKING

We often sit down at our computers with the intention of doing something useful. But it's actually the place where we tend to feel restless and distracted. And our concentration is getting worse. Research shows that when you work on a computer for an hour, your attention shifts more than eighty times. Back in 2004, that number was just twenty-four times an hour. So yes, our attention span is shrinking fast.

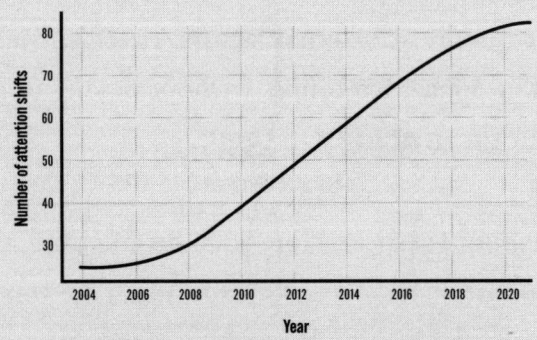

Changes to shifts in attention while working at a computer, 2004-2020
Source: *Attention Span: Finding Focus for a Fulfilling Life*, by Gloria Mark

In the following chapters, you'll get plenty of practical tips to repair concentration leaks, even if—or precisely because—your job involves working in a chaotic open office. You'll discover how to switch your focus ON, so you can put your foot on the gas when you really need to. Then we'll go over how to switch your focus OFF to help you properly recharge and get away from your to-do list—which is just as important.

THE BRAIN IN A NUTSHELL

Before we talk about the various ways to deal with concentration leaks, let's first look at how the brain works. We've made an easy model to show you where distractions come from and what you can do about them. In each of the following chapters, we'll zoom in on different parts of the model and repair the concentration leaks one by one.

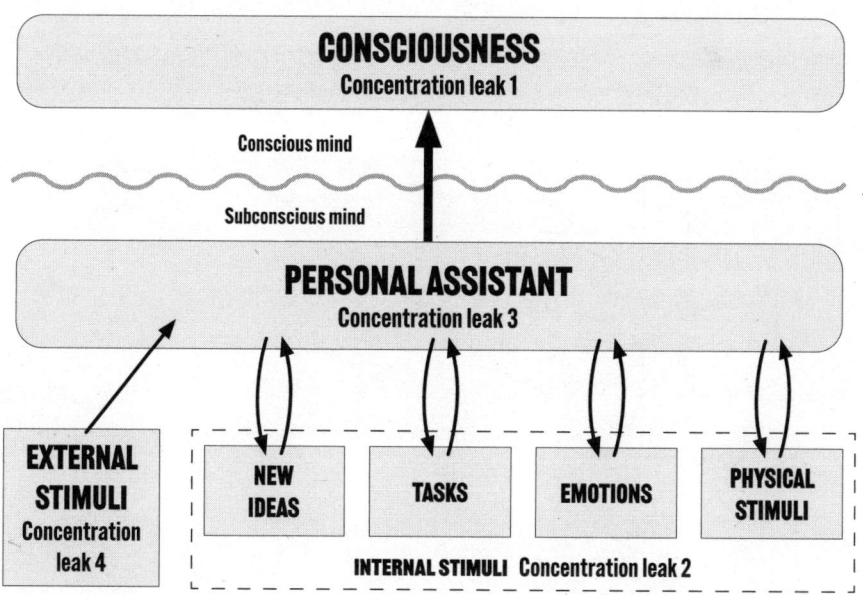

PART ONE

TARGETED ATTENTION AND THE FOUR CONCENTRATION LEAKS

CONCENTRATION LEAK 1

Too Few Stimuli

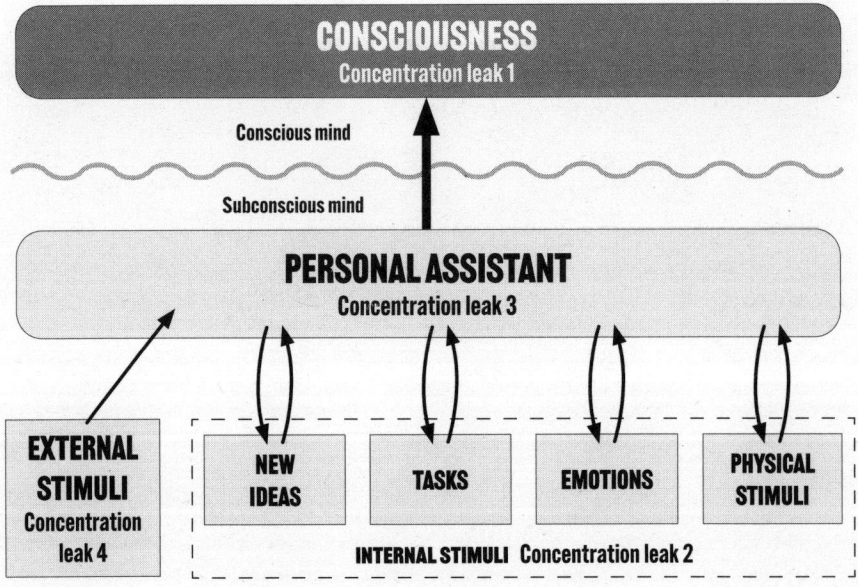

We can only do one thing consciously at a time, so use that attention wisely.

FOCUS CHALLENGE

Boredom

"Are you even listening?" my girlfriend asks me, her voice betraying her slight annoyance. It's not the first time my mind has wandered during one of our conversations. And she's right. I'm only half listening; new ideas keep popping up in my mind. I've been like this for as long as I can remember, and it means I'm often a little absent-minded, which annoys others and leaves me feeling guilty.

You might experience something similar when reading. While you're trying to get through a text, your mind is barraged with to-dos. Then, by the time you reach the end of the page, you realize you have no clue what you just read. Frustrating, right?

Another name for this is *mind wandering*: thinking about something other than what you're currently doing. We do this for almost half of our waking hours, proving exactly how limited our focus really is.[1]

The ability to think about things that aren't happening at the moment is a great cognitive skill; it's one of the things that set us apart from other animals. It does, however, come with a price tag: according to two Harvard researchers, it makes us unhappy.[2] It's the direct opposite of "living in the moment," and ultimately can prevent us from making deep connections with others.

Getting a grip on focus does more than just make you more efficient—it'll even make you happier! So how can you stop your mind from wandering? How do you stay attentive while you're reading or talking to someone? It's all a matter of creating flow.

OUR BRAINS THINK FASTER THAN WE USE THEM

Has anyone ever told you that we use only 10 percent of our brains? It's a total myth: we use the full 100 percent of our brain capacity.[3] In fact, that's precisely why we get distracted so easily.

Our minds are "on" virtually all the time. It's almost impossible for us not to think, and we do so at a constant, rapid pace. Estimates vary slightly, but it's believed our brains process information at a rate of about fourteen hundred words per minute. No wonder our thoughts are perpetually bouncing around in our brains.

Our thinking brain—the prefrontal cortex—is meant to run at 100 percent. If the task you're doing right now doesn't take up all of your available processing power, your personal assistant will start letting in other stimuli. It's a process that makes us efficient, but it also has a drawback: your brain is constantly on the hunt for new stimuli. Many of the tasks we do require only 20 percent of our brain capacity, leaving a lot of room for distraction.

The average reading rate, for example, is around 250 words per minute, which is significantly slower than the rate at which we think.[4] It's no wonder that our brains start thinking about other things when texts are a bit dry. Our brains simply have too much space left to use—a luxurious problem to have.

Clocking in at 125 words per minute, average speech speed is also well below our thinking speed, which means our minds are flooded with other stimuli while we talk.[5] You'll notice this most when you're on the phone with someone who's a fairly slow speaker. While they're trying to get to the point you reached two minutes ago, chances are you've doodled a rainforest's worth of trees on your notepad by the time they finally make their point.

If only a small part of your mind is occupied by tasks at hand, there's a lot more processing power left over to perceive other stimuli around you. As a result, you'll be much more distracted by things like coworkers making phone calls or people simply passing by.

To make matters worse, this is one situation where greater intelligence is actually a disadvantage. There's a clear correlation between your IQ and the capacity of your thinking brain.[6] The more intelligent you are, the greater your brain's capacity. Sure, it has its advantages, but the downside is that your mind finds it easier to think about other things when you're bored. Basically, the smarter you are, the more easily you're distracted.*

If you're looking to shut yourself off from distractions, here are two helping hands: noradrenaline and multitasking.

---

* Please take this as a compliment and use it in your favor when someone says you're easily distracted.

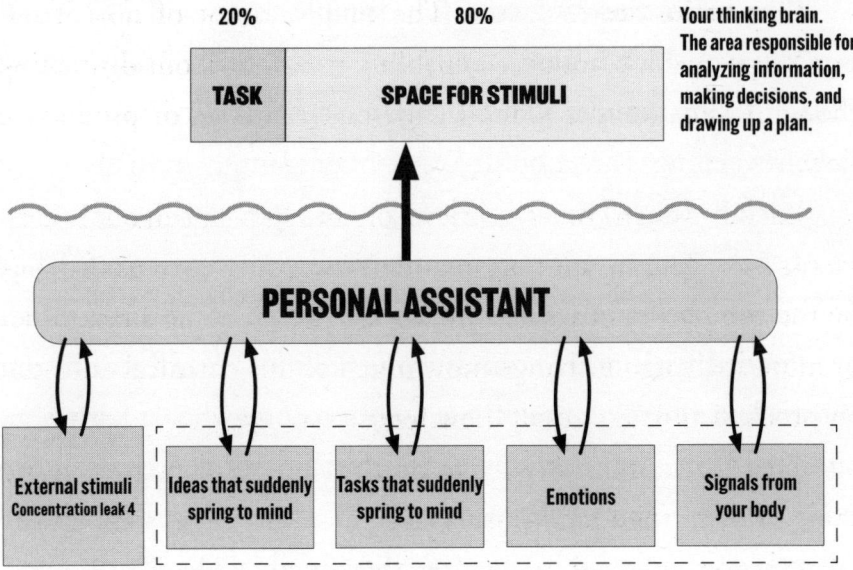

Your thinking brain is always 100 percent full. The question is with what? Is it the task itself, your own thoughts, or external stimuli? It's always a blend of all three areas. Because an average thinking task requires only 20 percent of our thinking capacity, there's plenty of space left to process other stimuli.

SHIFTING GEARS

Noradrenaline is a neurotransmitter that makes us pay more attention to what we're doing. It's like the brain's transmission. When our noradrenaline levels drop, our fast-moving minds get stuck in slow first gear and end up growing bored. On the flip side, when levels are too high, we experience grinding stress.

Imagine driving from New York to Philadelphia all on your own, in the dead of night, at 10 miles per hour. Chances are you'd fall asleep behind the wheel. Driving 160 miles per hour to stay awake, however, might not be the greatest idea either. The solution is somewhere in the middle.

Our brains are the same. The right amount of noradrenaline keeps us sharp and alert, enabling us to block out distracting thoughts and external stimuli and stay in a state of productive flow.*[7]

Luckily we can control the level of noradrenaline in our brains. Here's how: The amount of noradrenaline available to us depends on the complexity of what we're working on. Making a task easier or more challenging changes how much of this chemical our bodies produce and, as a result, how focused we are.

There are dozens of ways to do this. You've likely been using some of them for a long time. Have you ever put on some music

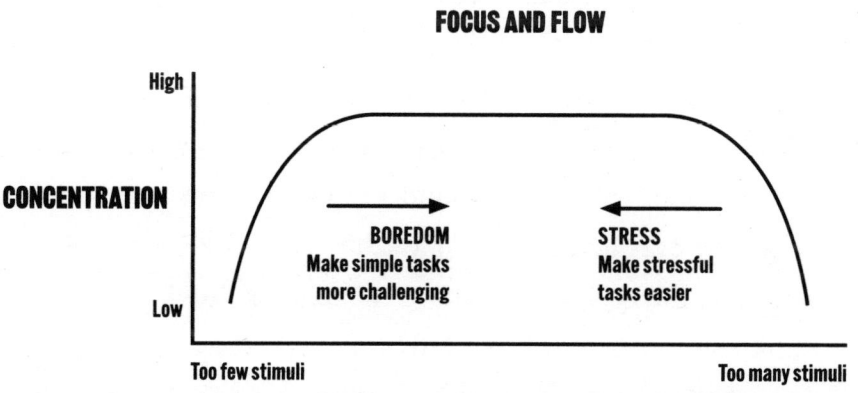

The Yerkes-Dodson law states that if we aren't stimulated enough we'll wander off, and that we become stressed when we're stimulated too much. The optimal state is in the middle: just enough challenge creates focus and flow.

---

* I was incredibly proud to have come up with this principle all on my own until a student pointed out to me that I'd been beaten to the punch by two gentlemen in 1908. Bummer. Alas, it's known as the Yerkes-Dodson law.

while driving? Why? Probably because without music, driving is too boring and easy. Listening to the radio gives your brain a new task to process, using up thinking power you have left over from driving, which takes more effort when you're bored. Strangely enough, music makes driving more enjoyable. Suppose, though, that you're trying to park in a tricky spot. Chances are the first thing you'll do is turn off the radio; when tasks become slightly more complicated, we prefer dealing with as few stimuli as possible. There are loads of ways to put this principle into practice.

FILLING THE VOID

I'm severely dyslexic, and reading used to be a serious struggle. As the slowest reader in my class, I found that my thoughts were given free rein to wander wherever they pleased. When I learned that reading stimulates only 20 percent of our brains, I started experimenting: every time I found my mind starting to wander, I moved my eyes across the lines a bit faster. By increasing my reading rate, the task became more challenging, leaving less room to think about other things. This drew me deeper into stories while boosting my focus, which made it much easier to absorb and remember information. This method works equally well both for people with dyslexia as well as for anyone else struggling with common tasks we encounter at work. It's a principle I call *filling the void*.

You can test this principle right away when reading. The idea is simple: Every time you notice your thoughts are wandering off or you're bothered by ambient noise, start reading a little faster. You don't have to change the way you read, just force your eyes to

| 20% TASK | 80% ROOM FOR DISTRACTION |

| 60% TASK | 40% ROOM FOR DISTRACTION |

The thinking brain is always completely occupied by a combination of the task at hand, internal stimuli, and external stimuli. Make the task more challenging, and there'll be less free space left for distractions.

move across the page a little faster. On the other hand, when the text becomes more difficult, try deliberately slowing down your reading speed.

You can use the same principle when giving presentations. For simple topics, deliberately speak a little faster than you normally would. Your audience will now have less free mental space to wander off and worry about the piles of emails they still have to plow through. They'll focus more on what you're trying to say, making it easier to remember the presentation.

Naturally, there's a limit to this. Speak too quickly and no one will understand what you're trying to say, significantly hindering comprehension. Funnily enough, it works exactly the same the other way around, too: speaking too slowly results in poor comprehension because people's minds tend to wander. It's all about striking a balance.

AVOID READING FROM SCREENS

As you might have noticed yourself, there's a difference between reading from paper and reading from a screen. Screens require far more effort, which is why our reading speeds drop by an average of 25 percent when we read digital texts, making it more difficult to stay focused.[8] Fortunately, there's a useful tool that makes reading from screens much easier: focusreader.com. This free PDF reader guides your eyes through texts, automatically increasing the speed at which you read the text to boost your concentration.

MULTITASKING AND TASK SWITCHING

Another way to make easy tasks slightly more challenging is to do another simple task on the side: doodling on a scrap of paper during a boring or slow phone conversation, for instance. Research by a British university found that these doodles increase our focus by 29 percent.[9] Why? They demand only a tiny amount of brain activity, so you'll have plenty of brain capacity left to process what's being said. Alternatively, they require just enough brainpower to block those pesky distracting thoughts: no more room for your to-do list means more attention given to the conversation.

But wait, isn't that multitasking? Yes, absolutely. To add even more fuel to the fire: Multitasking can be great for our focus and concentration. In fact, it's a key ingredient for achieving flow and becoming immersed in a task. This may sound at odds with the common yet outdated view that multitasking is something to be avoided at all costs. Quite the contrary; we should use it deliberately. But just as too much salt can ruin a perfectly good meal,

20% TASK	50% SIMPLE ACTIVITY	30% ROOM FOR DISTRACTION

When we can't make an easy task more complex ourselves, doing a second, simple task on the side can be quite helpful. This simple task fills the void, taking up space that would otherwise be filled by distracting thoughts or external stimuli.

mismanaged multitasking can leave you feeling stressed and cause you to make more mistakes. Knowing how this works—and when you should and should not multitask—can have a major impact on your focus.

First of all, know that there's a difference between multitasking and task switching. When we do two simple tasks at the same time, such as doodling and listening, we're multitasking. Task switching is something different: constantly alternating between two or more complex tasks. This is what happens when we try to quickly send an email about a different subject while we're on the phone. These switches are deceptively quick, making it seem as if we're doing two things at the same time, but hundreds of studies on the topic have shown that's not how it works. Instead, it results in a constant struggle with attention residue. We're more prone to error in both tasks, and it'll take us four to ten times longer to complete them.[10]

The key difference between multitasking and task switching is whether or not the side task requires targeted attention. If it does, we're task-switching. Game over.

Let's go back to the doodling example. Mindlessly scribbling on a piece of paper during an easy presentation is a great way to fill the void and improve your concentration. However, making elaborate 3D doodles with shading and shadowing tips the balance in the other direction. Elaborate drawings require targeted attention, causing you to switch between the two tasks at hand and miss information.

By default, our brains are set to multitasking. The only question is: Are you using it to your advantage?

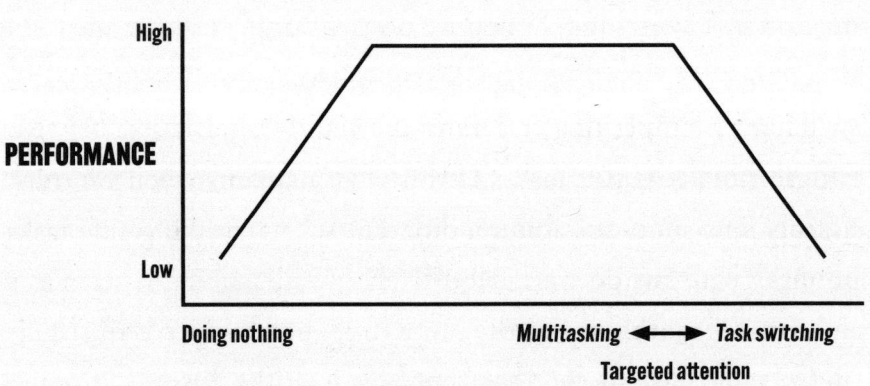

As soon as the side task starts requiring targeted attention, we lapse into task switching. When it doesn't, we're multitasking.

FOCUS BITE

OUT OF SIGHT, OUT OF MIND

Phone on silent with vibration off, but still right in front of you? Then it is still a distraction.

Your brain scans your surroundings about four times per second. This happens unconsciously, but it still uses brainpower. A phone is seen by your brain as something that might be important. If it is in sight, your brain stays alert to it, even if the sound and vibration are turned off.

The farther away your phone is, the less it distracts you. How easily you get distracted depends on the person and the situation. But if you need to focus deeply on a task or conversation, take your phone off your desk or out of your pocket and put it somewhere else.

You can go a step further than just putting your phone out of sight. Clear your desk as well. If your brain doesn't see loose papers and unfinished tasks, it will not be distracted by them either.

Here's a simple rule of thumb: If you notice you're doing two things at once, you're task-switching. If you don't, you're multitasking. The most suitable candidates for multitasking side tasks are tasks you can do on autopilot, like walking while making a phone call. Another example:

Do you ever listen to music at work?

Do you think that's good or bad for your brain?

Well, it depends on what you're listening to. If you're listening to music that you've heard a thousand times before, it'll do wonders for your brain. Our brains don't pay much conscious attention to music it already knows. This makes listening to familiar music a great way to fill the void, helping us to fully focus on the task at hand. I wrote 90 percent of this book listening to one long playlist, over and over again. It isn't boring; it is focus.

But when your favorite artist just released a new album and you decide to put it on while cranking out a boring report, that's a different story. There's a good chance that your mind will wander off to focus on the music. Result: a cognitive shift, forcing you back to square one.

How about driving a car and talking on the phone at the same time? Are they easy to combine? I can only guess your answer right now, but there are some interesting stats I can share. Eighty-eight percent of motorists view other drivers making phone calls and texting while driving as a serious threat to their safety. Yet 80 percent of those very motorists admit to using their phones while driving, without feeling that doing so affects their ability to drive safely.[11]

The fact is that both driving and using our phones require targeted attention. Doing both simultaneously means you're switching between the two. And we tend to overestimate our own abilities when we do tasks like these.

Some people think that hands-free calling is a good alternative, but this couldn't be further from the truth. Sure, it allows us to keep our hands on the steering wheel, but that's not the bottleneck. Our brains are. When we are having a call, our brains need to process it, leaving much less thinking power to process traffic and therefore causing us to react more slowly to our surroundings.

WHY WE CAN'T STUDY AND READ AT THE SAME TIME

Even trying to remember information while reading requires us to task-switch. This is because we'll always have to do something to store the information in our long-term memory. Some people reread texts, others take notes, and others highlight important passages.* Whatever your strategy, the process is different from reading; committing information to memory always involves two tasks. Since both actions demand targeted attention, they interfere with each other.[12]

Basically, the more we focus on remembering a text while reading, the more time it'll take to absorb the text. It's the same in the other direction: the more we focus on actually reading a text, the less we'll remember. If you've ever realized after reading something that you don't remember a single thing about it, and you feel like your memory isn't much better than a gaping sieve, chances are you were simply trying to read and remember at the same time.

We can consciously do only one thing at a time.

---

* Oddly enough, research has shown highlighting to be the least effective way to remember something. It's too passive, which means the information is never actually stored in our brains.

My advice is to separate reading from remembering. When reading, just try to understand the information at first. If there's something you don't understand, reread the passage, look it up, or go back a few pages if necessary. Only after you finish absorbing the information should you start to store the information in your memory. It's important to realize that this doesn't take more time; it's just a different way of organizing your time. Turn the pattern of read/remember/read/remember into read/read/remember/remember. Fewer switches, less attention residue, less effort, way more effective. It's win-win.

GOING FOR A WALK

Our brains need stimuli to perform well, but when there are too many stimuli we start to stress, and our performance takes a hit. You can actually use this to your benefit: limiting the space available for distractions helps you be more present in the moment. You'll find it a lot easier to absorb and process information, and you'll connect better with people you're talking to.

My girlfriend and I make a habit of taking a walk together every night while we catch up. The simple act of walking together helps us (okay, me) avoid getting distracted, and makes it easier for me to stay present in the moment.

PRACTICAL TIPS FOR BATTLING BOREDOM, OR TOO FEW STIMULI

Tip 1: Avoid Distraction by Working Faster

- ✓ Avoiding distractions from coworkers by working faster is a great way to shut yourself off from external stimuli.
- ✓ When coworkers talking just a little too loudly on the phone distract you from your work, this is generally a sign that what you're doing is too easy for your brain. Fill that space by making the task at hand just a little more challenging.
- ✓ There are lots of different ways to make a task more difficult, but here are some examples:
  - Give yourself simple deadlines: if task X usually takes sixty minutes, try to do it in fifty-five.
  - During overly simple or boring meetings, give yourself basic assignments: I want everyone to feel heard, I want to speak as calmly as possible, or I want to pay more attention to nonverbal communication, etc.
  - Type a little faster.
  - When working on overly simple or boring reports, try to embellish your writing even if it isn't necessary.

Tip 2: Cleaning Powers the Brain

- ✓ A friend told me that when he's really busy at work, he tends to clean his house. "When I want to really focus and home in on a project, the simple task of cleaning gives me peace of mind. It frees me from all my distracting thoughts and gives me the mental space I need to really think about the project," he told me. In essence, this is a practical manifestation of the "filling the void" principle.

Tip 3: Paper Clips as Conversation Helpers

- ✓ Fidgeting with something in your hands while having a conversation can be a great way to keep your mind occupied. This works especially well with objects that you're not too familiar with, meaning not your keys or your phone. For example, I often carry a paper clip or a little pebble in my pocket to fiddle with as I talk. It might sound a bit weird, but it works.

FOCUS BITE

DOES FIDGETING HELP YOU FOCUS?

At Auckland University of Technology, MRI scans were used to study what happens in the brain when you fidget. And that goes far beyond playing with a Pop-It or spinner (if you're not familiar, ask your kid, your neighbor's daughter, or your nephew).

It also includes tapping your toes, rocking back on your chair, biting your nails, drumming your fingers, clicking a pen, playing with your jewelry, pacing around the office, tearing up coasters at the bar, running your hands through your hair, rubbing your fingers together, and so on.

The key finding: When you fidget, more blood flows to your prefrontal cortex.

Most tasks use only about 20 percent of our brain capacity. Because our brains are built to run at 100 percent, they automatically start looking for extra stimuli. Fidgeting fills some of that empty space. This only works for tasks that are naturally simple.

When a task really demands your full attention, like a difficult conversation, you don't need to fidget.

Holding something that creates a predictable rhythm can also feel calming. That can be helpful in stressful situations. It doesn't matter if you're tapping your feet, clicking your pen, or pacing around the room. What matters is that you're doing something that doesn't require targeted attention.

That's why walking while making a phone call works so well for many people.

And yes, it does matter what task you pair it with. You can never consciously do two things at the same time. Walking happens on autopilot, which leaves room to focus on the call. But try drawing a circle in the air with your left hand while drawing a square with your right. Doesn't work, right? That's because both actions require conscious thought.

CONCENTRATION LEAK 2

Too Many Internal Stimuli

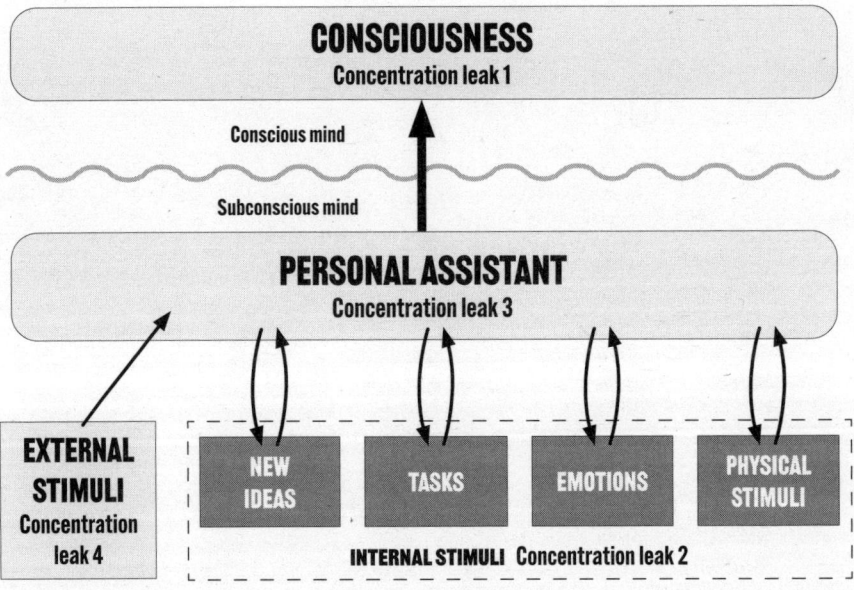

The biggest distraction is not the world around you, but the world inside your head.

FOCUS CHALLENGE

Overscheduling and Overcommitting

If you came into my office a few years ago, you'd have found an avalanche of Post-its of all the projects I was working on. I guess I worked on around twenty-five projects at the same time, and I loved it. There was always something to do, and I was never bored. I was successful and busy all the time.

At least, that's what I told myself. In reality, I was mostly stressed. And to be honest, I'd be lying if I said I was productive. Despite the fact there weren't any colleagues distracting me, I'd spend the whole day bouncing from one task to another: writing a marketing plan, reading an article, having a meeting, starting up a new exciting project. It was the exact opposite of focus, which my friends were all too happy to point out to me.

I also started to realize that my projects rarely made it to the finish line. If I couldn't find a way out, I'd just continue with another (more fun) project. I'd tell myself it was a break of sorts; if I spent just a little time working on something fun, I could recharge and find new energy to tackle the difficult project I was working on earlier. More often than not, I failed to return to the difficult projects, which meant they were left hanging.

During that time, I met some entrepreneurs who were a few steps ahead of me. Most of them focused on just one activity at a time and took their time to get it right. As a result, they worked fewer hours, were considerably more relaxed, and even made more money. They were clear about their main task, focused only on that task, and considered everything else a distraction. Clearly I had a lot to learn.

MAGPIES AT WORK

Our brains naturally prefer everything new and exciting.[1] Back when we were still living in caves, this was a useful tendency because it encouraged us to explore the world around us. A friend of mine calls this "magpie behavior": if it's shiny and interesting, it'll immediately grab our attention. Unfortunately, we never shook off that urge, which is why we often think it's a good idea to suddenly drop everything in the middle of working through spreadsheets and open up CNN to check for news updates. As a result of "magpie behavior," our work is becoming more and more fragmented.

Our constant hunt for new stimuli causes us to frequently switch from one task to the next, giving us the impression that we're productive. There's actually a proven correlation between the number of projects we're working on and how well we're able to focus. Unsurprisingly, it's a negative correlation; the more projects we work on simultaneously, the more our concentration and productivity suffers.

This is how it works: When we're working on lots of different projects at once, we naturally encounter considerably more external distractors. While working on project A, we'll also receive emails about projects B and C, along with requests to participate in an emergency meeting about project D, never mind all the other minor questions we have to field about the projects. Despite these external distractors, it's the increase in internal distractors that affects our focus the most. While we're working on project A, we suddenly come up with a solution to a problem with project C, quickly followed by a reminder that there's still some work to be done for project B. Working on too many different projects simultaneously guarantees constant attention residue and, thus, poor focus.

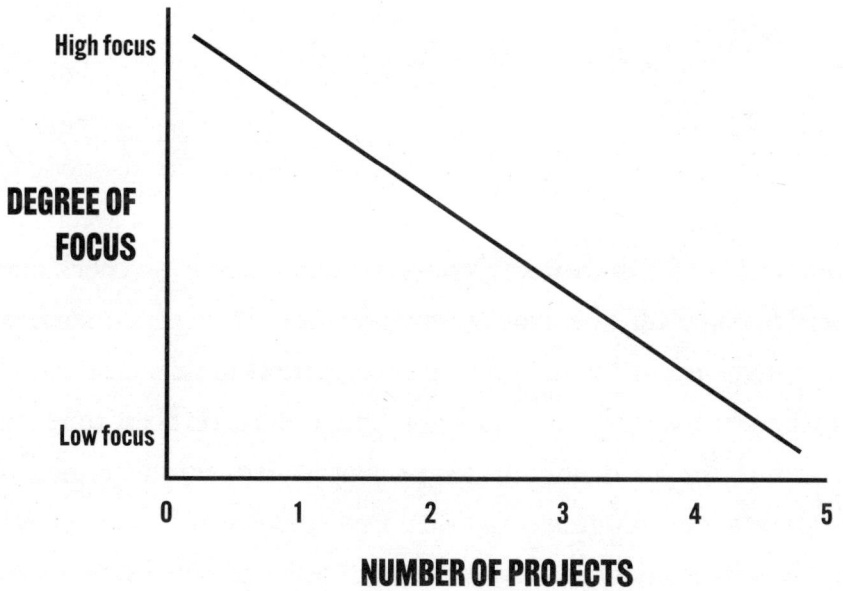

My colleague Chris Bailey thought of a simple, yet striking graph to show the correlation between our focus and the number of projects we're working on.[2]

According to Gloria Mark, a professor at the University of California, Irvine, who has researched the subject thoroughly, "on average, we switch between tasks and projects forty-eight times a day, prompted only by ourselves." These cognitive shifts cost us a lot of effort, and make it more difficult to dive deep into a task. The minute we start struggling with a particular task, we'll just shift to another, slightly easier task. After all, that's the path of least resistance. You probably know the feeling: you've just gotten going, but then you get stuck on something difficult, and switch to surfing the internet or shooting off some easy emails instead.

> When we're working on the computer, we shift from one task to another an average of 566 times a day. That's the equivalent of once every fifty seconds.[3]

Here's another fun fact: there's a clear relationship between the number of projects we're involved in and how often we check our social media feeds.[4] It's a fairly easy phenomenon to explain; when we're involved in lots of projects, we're interrupted more often. This results in attention residue, making it more difficult to really delve into the depths of a single project. When we're working on many different things at once, we'll never achieve full focus, so it's hardly surprising that we instead turn to easier activities like scrolling through social media.

TEST IT YOURSELF

HOW DISTRACTING IS YOUR PHONE?

Have you felt the urge to check your phone or email while reading this book? You're certainly not the only one. It's worth keeping track of how often you check your phone while in the middle of another task, both when you're at home and when you're at work. If you're looking to cut down on how often you check your phone, the plus-five rule can be a great help. The rule works like this: every time you feel the need to check your phone or email, tell yourself you have to wait five minutes. You'll train yourself to gradually increase your attention span.

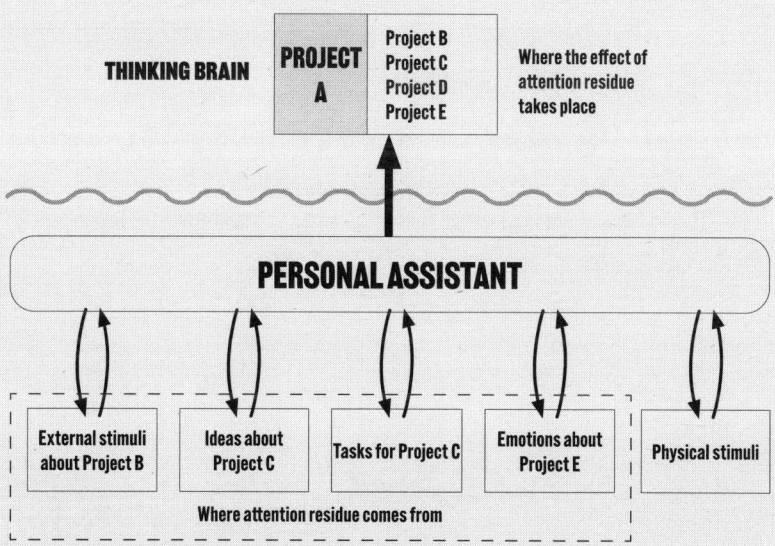

When we're working on lots of projects at once, attention residue occupies a large share of our subconscious minds.

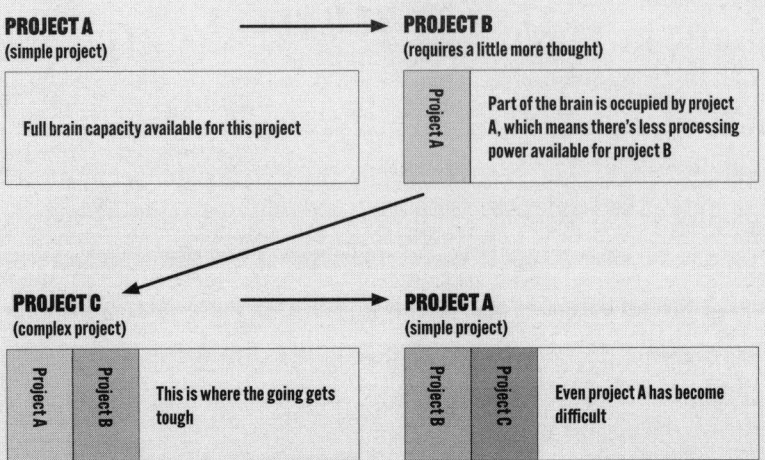

The more complex the task or project, the longer it lingers in our minds after we switch to focus on something else. As a result, our minds gradually fill up as our thinking power and focus decline. Even a task as simple as project A becomes difficult because a large part of our minds are occupied by other projects.

Small disclaimer: This does depend on how actively you're involved with the projects. A friend of mine owns six different companies, but operationally he does "as little as possible." There's nothing wrong with that. Think of it like flying a helicopter: the higher you fly, the more you'll be able to see, at the expense of minute details.

MTS: MINIMIZE TASK SWITCHING

Minimizing task switching improves our focus. When you're just getting started, it may feel a little uncomfortable because you're not getting the rush from bouncing from one task to another. That rush is precisely the problem: our brains are addicted to finding new stimuli. Every time we shift to a new task, it produces chemicals that make us feel good and keep up the behavior. We'll talk about this issue in more detail later on.

When you start cutting down on task switching, it's not unusual to experience some withdrawal symptoms at first (it sounds more intense than it really is). Practically speaking, you may feel a little restless. Most people do; it's completely normal. It's just a phase you have to get through. At the same time, you'll see your productivity improve by leaps and bounds, helping you get more done and go home feeling satisfied with your day. The most successful people I know made the practice of minimizing task switching into a veritable art form and take a systematic approach to it. There are many ways you can do the same.

Grouping Tasks

The simplest way to reduce how often you switch tasks is to group tasks. Usually this involves grouping tasks on a project-by-project basis: I'll only work on project A in the morning, then move to project B after lunch. But because projects usually consist of a set of different tasks such as reading, meetings, writing, phone calls, etc., our brains will still be task switching when working this way. The subject doesn't really matter to our brains; what matters is the activity. That's why a more effective approach is to group tasks by brain activity. For example, schedule all writing tasks in the morning and all phone calls in the afternoon.

> **It would be weird to wash all your clothes separately, and the same applies to your tasks. It always takes some time to get going, so grouping tasks is a great help.**

You could also devote more time to your main task. For instance, you can plan to spend all your time between 10 a.m. and 3 p.m. landing new clients or writing a major research report. Less important tasks you can do either before or after that time slot.

This might seem boring at first, as your body won't produce as many feel-good chemicals. But because of the significant increase in productivity you'll experience, you'll ultimately go home feeling satisfied more often. Time to bite the bullet and stop rushing!

Setting Theme Days

When you want to take grouping tasks to the next level, you should work in theme days, which were tremendously helpful to me when I was writing this book. I found out about theme days from entrepreneur Charlotte van 't Wout. She runs two companies and as a business influencer shares lots of tips on productivity and entrepreneurship on Instagram.

"To avoid being overwhelmed by the sheer number of different tasks I could do in one day, I give themes to my days. For example, I schedule all my appointments on Friday. This creates worlds of peace and quiet. Otherwise, here's what happens: Suppose I'm going to meet someone for coffee at 10:30 a.m. on Tuesday. But at 9 a.m. I think perhaps it's time to get started on that important task I've been putting off. I have to shoot that down because I know I need to leave by 10 a.m. to make it to the coffee place on time. Instead of working, I end up wasting my free hour, followed by a coffee date. By the time I get back to work, it's 12:30 p.m., meaning it's almost time for lunch. That's how a single coffee date can swallow up an entire morning."

Thanks to her "social Fridays," Charlotte can focus on other tasks the rest of the week without being distracted. "Plus it means I'm no longer preoccupied with some project I was working on five minutes ago. I can enjoy my cup of coffee and give my full attention to the people I'm meeting with," she added.

Like Charlotte, Oscar and I have also structured our workdays into themes. It's an approach that works well for us. It provides rhythm and clarity. Much less piecemeal and more tranquility. Less task switching and, therefore, more productive. Currently, our themes look like the tables at the top of page 46.

Our themes are not set in stone; we see them more as guidelines. If an important person can meet only on Thursday morning, I will accommodate that. But that's more the exception than the rule.

You can also choose to allocate themes to particular weeks or months. In the past, for instance, I'd read every single book recommended to me and listen to all the podcasts I found interesting.

Mark's Themes

MONDAY	TUESDAY	WEDNESDAY	THURSDAY	FRIDAY
Weekly Meeting	Writing	Writing	Writing	Appointments
Projects	Minor Tasks	Reading	Reading	Appointments

My current weekly schedule. It differs from quarter to quarter, but because writing this book is currently my number one priority it's the project I'm emphasizing most, in addition to reading scientific papers.

Oscar's Themes

MONDAY	TUESDAY	WEDNESDAY	THURSDAY	FRIDAY
Team Meeting	Deep Work	Team Meeting	Deep Work	Creative Work
Shallow Work	Deep Work	Shallow Work	Deep Work	Creative Work

Shallow work: finances, emails, small projects, snacks. Deep work: reading, writing, research, programming, major projects. Creative work: recording podcasts or company videos, brainstorming.

But this filled my mind with ideas about marketing, whereas I was supposed to be preparing a podcast about the brain. These days, I've started theming what I read and listen to as well, picking one new subject to study in-depth every month. At the moment that's nutrition, which means I'm reading books and listening to podcasts about only that topic this month. It's made me a lot more relaxed, and because I'm fully immersed in the subject, I absorb the content faster.

Working in Sprints

This idea of grouping tasks can also be applied to projects. A few years ago, for example, I had to update our company's pension plan. It's not something I was super excited to do, but it was an inescapable task. Via a friend, I ended up working with a pension consultancy with the tagline "We know you don't feel like doing this, so we'll get everything done in a day." It was a perfect match.

They visited the office and, true to their word, they got everything done within one day. Afterward, the pension consultant told me how they used to work on at least five clients at once. "We had to constantly switch from one task to another and lost a lot of time traveling. Because we now dedicate all our attention to one client at a time, we never have to deal with the same issue twice. Which, ultimately, means we finish faster."

It's an idea that goes against conventional wisdom. We grew up with the idea that parallel work is more efficient. Sure, that's true if machines are the ones doing all the work; they don't have to deal with attention residue the way we do. When we switch between tasks, it takes 50 percent longer to complete the various tasks at hand than if we just work on one task at a time.[5] In other words: when it comes to brainwork, linear work is more efficient than parallel work.

At Focus Academy, we try to schedule our projects one after the other wherever possible, rather than working on them all simultaneously. It doesn't always work out as planned, but we usually manage. The exception to this is that customer contact does run in parallel, though we try to organize the actual projects with customers linearly so we can focus on one at a time.

Kill Your Darlings

Another approach that can help you reduce task switching is doing less. This is also known as the 25/5 rule. The idea is simple. Make a list of your twenty-five most important life goals. Now circle the five most important ones. The rest should be avoided. To achieve those five goals, you have to ignore the other twenty.

Skipping things you don't like is easy. The hard part is ignoring the things you find fun and interesting, but that aren't exactly in line with your goals.

The same principle applies to to-do lists. We usually have more to-dos than we have time. Crossing off every item on the list should never be your goal, tempting as it is; it's fighting a losing battle. What matters most is what you choose not to do.

When we turn it around and consider everything we can do, we're tempted to prioritize minor tasks just for the sake of ticking boxes. The Germans even have a word for this: *Entlistungsfreude*, the joy we feel when we can cross off items on our to-do lists. We love this feeling so much that we even add tasks to our to-do lists that we've already finished just so we can tick them off. Recognizable? Yeah, you're not the only one.

However, this approach encourages us to avoid—or at least postpone—tasks that really matter, which usually require a bit more effort. In one of my interviews with Tony Crabbe, who authored the best-selling book *Busy: How to Thrive in a World of Too Much*, he told me "To-do lists are an awful way to structure your day." When we take an unfiltered glance at our to-do lists, it's easy to become overwhelmed. Instead, it's much more effective to ask yourself at the start of the day, What do I need to do today to make sure I go home satisfied? "Make a top three of your most important goals and do them first," Crabbe advised.

> ### THIS IS HOW MARK WORKS
>
> From heavy to light. The first two hours of my day are my focus hours. That's when I tackle the most important tasks. No matter what happens, I know I've already done the most essential work. In the afternoon, I shift to tasks that require less brainpower.

> ### THIS IS HOW OSCAR WORKS
>
> Together with my colleagues at Focus Academy, we work in six-week sprints. After the sprint, we take two weeks to slow down, reflect on the previous sprint, and prepare for the next one. This "pause" also gives us extra space for creative projects and deeper work. Then we kick off the next sprint with fresh energy.

Closing the Loop: The OHIO Principle

Time for another task-switching culprit: open loops. I'm sure you know this situation well: You're about to head into a meeting, but decide to quickly check your email first. You scroll through your inbox, read a few emails, then enter the meeting room. What does this do to your brain?

If we don't complete a task, it lingers in our minds and saps energy, leaving an open loop. When the meeting starts, your brain is still processing the emails you just read, attention residue making it less alert and less sharp. To make matters worse, when the meeting ends, you have to return to the emails a second time.

You can significantly increase your effectiveness by using the OHIO principle, which stands for Only Handle It Once. The core tenet of this principle is to create as few open loops as possible. It consists of two components:

1. Don't Start a Task That You Can't Finish

If you already know you won't have much time to work on a task, it's wiser to avoid starting in the first place. If you check your phone for new messages right before a meeting, you risk ending up in an open loop. If you can't finish a minor task immediately, just don't do it. It'll take up precious thinking power.

For example, a while ago I realized I often read my emails on my phone, but rarely responded from my phone. When I returned to the office later in the day, I'd open my laptop and check my inbox a second time, reading and responding to emails I already read. Now I no longer read my emails on my phone. I've literally halved the time I spend on my inbox, and I'm considerably more mindful in the present. I can focus on my emails and handle them immediately, rather than leaving them to clog up my inbox or marking them "unread" to make sure I don't forget them.

2. Complete Tasks as Quickly as Possible

You also experience open loops when you move on to new tasks, meetings, or projects without finishing what you were working on first. According to the OHIO principle, you should aim to complete tasks as quickly as possible. One of my clients told me how this principle helped them to significantly improve their efficiency: "These days, we schedule some time right after our meetings to do some of the actions discussed. Seeing as they have to be done anyway, this approach means I don't have to worry about them anymore. We're getting an incredible number of positive customer reactions because of it; they really appreciate how quickly we address action points."

Since adopting the OHIO principle, I've cleared my wall of Post-its and now work only on one major project at a time. I still have a tendency to say "yes!" to everything, but luckily I can rely on the great group of people around me to subtly remind me that doing everything at once does not help my focus. I take their hints and neatly park new projects until I've finished whatever I'm currently working on. Definitely an improvement for me.

PRACTICAL TIPS TO MITIGATE BUSYNESS OR TOO MANY INTERNAL STIMULI

Tip 1: Don't Start Anything Right Before a Meeting
- ✓ Get into the habit of steering clear of your phone right before meetings. It'll be a bit uncomfortable at first, but you'll soon notice that you're more focused during meetings.

Tip 2: Reduce Task Switching with Theme Days
- ✓ Determine which themes or projects matter most to you, then block off time for them in your calendar. You don't have to apply this to your whole week; even one morning or afternoon a week can help. Experiment to figure out what works for you.

Tip 3: Find More Peace of Mind with a Not-to-Do List
- ✓ Start by listing temptingly fun or interesting tasks and projects that you just can't get around to at the moment. It's best to park them for the time being. Focus. Finish what you were doing first.

FOCUS CHALLENGE

A Cluttered Mind

A while back, I had the honor of giving a TEDx Talk in Curaçao about how focus can influence perception. When I was done, right as I was about to take my first well-deserved sip of a cocktail, a woman came up to me. "Can I ask you a quick question?" she inquired. "Of course," I replied, knowing that when that's how the conversation starts, it's going to be a while before I can enjoy my drink.

"When I'm in the office, I often find myself running into desks or even people," she started. "It's like I don't see them. And when I'm walking down the street with my teenaged daughter, she has to stop me from getting hit by cars and mopeds. Do you have any idea why this is?" She'd already had her eyes checked, and they turned out to be fine. We continued talking, and after some time it became clear that she always has a lot on her mind. Even after work, her mind would keep spinning, and she had a hard time not thinking about everything she still had to do. "That's exactly why I struggle to fall asleep at night; my mind is still in sixth gear. Sometimes I wake up in the middle of the night because I've just remembered something I have to do the next day." This seemed to me an important clue to her constant battle with inanimate objects.

JUGGLING TOO MANY BALLS

We think all day long. It's estimated that we have about fifty thousand individual thoughts a day, and it's common to grow tired of being a 24/7 thinking machine. There are times we want to empty our minds and not think at all. Unfortunately, an empty mind is impossible; luckily, you don't need one.

After all, we're not distracted by every single thought. We mainly suffer from thoughts that keep flying back like boomerangs, such as an uneasy conversation or tasks that are still on our to-do lists. All these open loops can fill up our minds, making it more difficult to fall asleep. And in exceptional cases, they can even affect perception.

This is how it works: Suppose I ask you to juggle three balls. With a little practice, you can do it. But when I give you a fourth ball, the task will quickly become a lot harder. By the time I add a fifth ball, balls will probably be flying everywhere.

Our heads work in the same way: the more balls we try to keep in the air, the more likely we are to make mistakes. Every time we realize there's another task we have to do, we're juggling an extra mental ball, which works like an enormous attention magnet.

Imagine you and I are talking. During our chat, I suddenly

remember that I still have to go to the store to pick up pasta sauce. It might seem like a trivial task, but if I forget I'll be subjected to a depressingly dry dinner. The personal assistant in my mind will see it as an "emergency task," demanding my attention and removing me forcefully from the conversation: "Don't forget to pick up that pasta sauce later!"

Part of my mind is now occupied with remembering that task, leaving less free space for the conversation I am having with you. This is what makes my head feel literally full. I'm trying to juggle one ball too many.

The more effort I put into getting back into the conversation, the more my other task will fade into the background. It's a gradual process, during which I'm left with attention residue all the same. Part of my mind is still preoccupied with Operation: Pasta Sauce, whereas the other part is processing our conversation.

Until I make time to actually go and buy the pasta sauce, my personal assistant will keep reminding me not to forget. You may recognize this all-too-frequent loop and understand how exhausting it can be. Have you ever noticed how your brain has a tendency

30% GET PASTA SAUCE	70% ATTENTION FOR THE CONVERSATION

When you cling to small tasks in your mind, you're left with less free space for the task at hand.

to remind you of these things at completely illogical moments? While you stand in line for the checkout counter, your brain suddenly brings up a reminder that you've still got a report to read, or jogs your memory to tell you about tomorrow's important phone call while you're lying in bed. Not particularly practical.

To your mind, this whole process is no different from a phone call interrupting your conversation; your mind doesn't discriminate between internal and external distractors. That's why it's hard to fall asleep when you're constantly being reminded about tasks that you absolutely shouldn't forget tomorrow. It's like getting constant notifications on your phone.

The more you use your mind to remember small tasks, the more it'll distract you. This is exactly what was going on with the

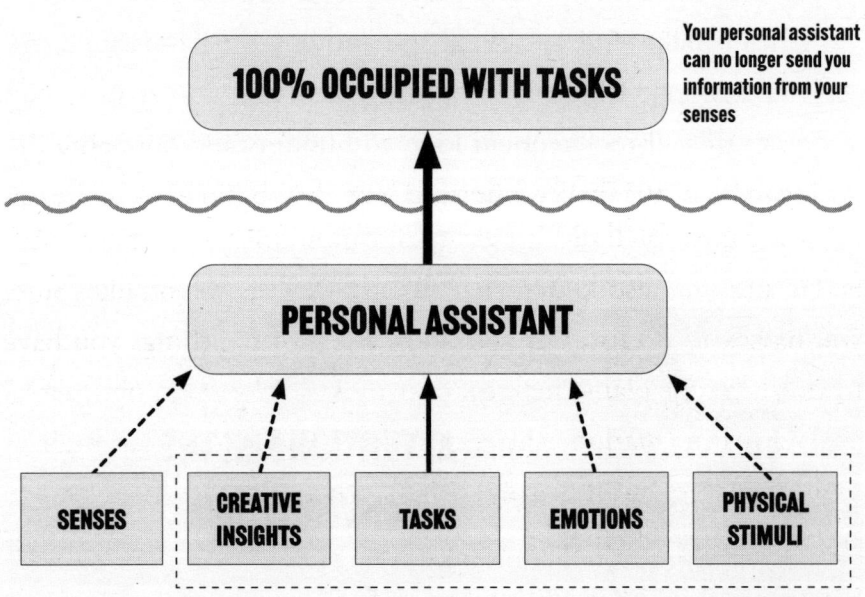

Because your thinking brain is full of tasks, there's less space to transmit sensory information.

woman who kept banging into desks: because she was constantly thinking about everything she had to do, she completely filled up her thinking brain to the point that there was literally no more room in her mind for other things. Her eyes had no problem seeing desks, but her brain just wasn't registering them. This is called *inattentional blindness*: because our attention is limited, we can't see what's happening right before our eyes.[1] This is the same tactic magicians use to make rabbits disappear in front of us.

AN EXTERNAL HARD DRIVE FOR YOUR BRAIN

Unfortunately, we can't change anything about the limited capacity of one of the most important parts of our brains. Our brains are still capable of fantastic feats, but only if we accept and work with their limitations. If we don't, the bucket will overflow and we'll make mistakes or need more energy to complete tasks.

Oddly enough, in my experience, highly educated people are more prone to overloading their brains. The more intelligent you are, the more you'll do things in your mind. Sure, you have a calendar, but you also know what the next few days look like. Sure, you have a to-do list, but you know most of the things you have to do: creating plans, making decisions, tracking appointments, analyzing information, setting priorities, and so on. Your brain is highly capable, but it usually comes with a price tag. Some people are exhausted when they come home from work, while others struggle to fully focus during meetings.

This is why many people tend to deal with incoming tasks right away, on the pretext of getting them "out of their mind."

Although there's nothing wrong with this line of thought—it can be a perfectly adequate strategy—it can also make you a slave to anything that pings or dings, preventing you from diving deep. It can make work very erratic.

Fortunately, there's an alternative: a method to make incoming tasks easier to deal with, so you can experience more peace of mind during the day. A method to help you take the plunge, even when hundreds of tasks are flying at you at once. Neuropsychologists call it *cognitive distribution*. Fancy phrase, but what is it? Well, technically, it's just a sophisticated way of saying "pen and paper." The more thoughts and tasks we off-load from our minds, the more space we free up to analyze information and make decisions. Writing down our thoughts is like putting information on an external hard drive.

The best-known example of cognitive distribution is our calendars. Our minds would be chaotic if we didn't have a place to write down our appointments, and had to keep track of them in our minds instead. Calendars give clarity and peace of mind because they save us from juggling all the mental balls by ourselves. Another example: Do you ever send yourself emails about things you shouldn't forget? Cognitive distribution.

A friend of mine does the same by leaving himself voicemail messages: "Hi, Ben, it's me again. Book your flight today."

These peculiar habits all serve the same purpose: emptying our heads to create space. Once we've emptied our minds of a task, we don't have to think about it until later, which has more advantages than you might think.

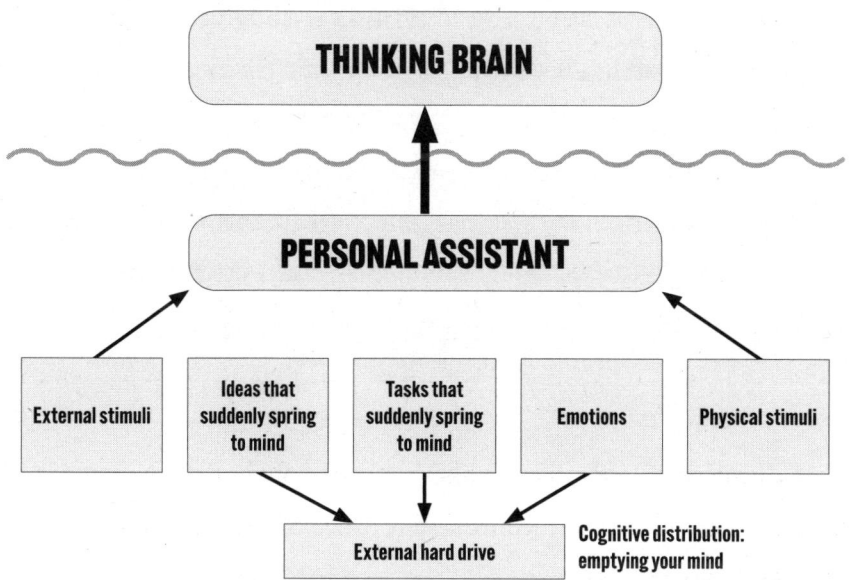

By emptying your mind of tasks and ideas, you can reduce the workload of your personal assistant, making it less likely to interrupt you.

FOCUS AND CALM THROUGH COGNITIVE DISTRIBUTION

Distracting external stimuli and distracting thoughts are blocked by an area of the brain called the *ventrolateral prefrontal cortex*, or VLPFC for short.[2] This part of the brain is located in the same area as your thinking brain, so the two parts have to compete for energy. The fuller your thinking brain, the worse your VLPFC will function, and the faster you'll be distracted. In other words, the emptier your mind, the better you can focus.

An empty mind also makes it easier to switch from one task to another, such as when someone interrupts you.[3] It's no surprise that an empty mind doesn't weigh you down as much.

> The area in your brain that determines how well you regulate emotions and perform under pressure is known as the *ventromedial prefrontal cortex*. This area also makes up part of your thinking brain. As your thinking brain fills up with things it can't forget, you become less capable of regulating your emotions and keeping stress at bay. Giving a presentation to a large audience, for instance, becomes more difficult if your head is full of trivialities, such as all the groceries you still have to buy.

Cognitive distribution makes us more resilient. The goal here is to develop this principle and use it more often. There are various ways to do so.

EMPTY YOUR HEAD TO ACCOMPLISH MORE

The founder of this principle is David Allen, who worked as a productivity consultant for corporations in the 1980s. He noticed that the amount of stress you experience doesn't necessarily depend on how much you have on your plate. "Two people doing exactly the same work under the same conditions can experience stress in completely different ways. One may be completely overwhelmed, whereas the other will thrive. Strangely enough, this difference cannot be explained by intelligence or experience. How much stress you experience is largely due to how many tasks you're holding on to in your mind. We use our head as an office, and that's not what it was made for," Allen says.

He found that when people empty their minds, they get far more done, and more importantly, experience less stress. Based on this idea, he developed his famed Getting Things Done (GTD) method.[4] The five steps in the GTD method are (1) Capture, (2) Clarify, (3) Organize, (4) Reflect, (5) Engage.

He was clearly ahead of his time, as scientists only recently found proof for the principles he devised forty years ago.[5]

Here is evidence that the principles work: The moment you recommend something to him, such as a good book, movie, or restaurant, he'll take his notebook and write it down (capture). This empties his head, giving him peace of mind, allowing him to focus fully on the conversation at hand (engage). Later, he rewrites the note (clarify) and parks it on the right list (organize). In his weekly review, he goes through all his lists to clean them up (reflect). Despite flying all over the world to give lectures and having a rather busy schedule, there's still nothing on his mind. He's always fully present. "There's a difference between being busy and feeling busy," Allen told me.

He's now well into his seventies, but every time I see him, I'm struck by how dapper he looks. I suppose he has good genes, but I also suspect that not holding on to anything in his mind plays a big part. Emptying your mind on a regular basis is one of the healthiest things you can do for your brain.

FOCUS BITE

HOW DO YOU CLEAR YOUR HEAD?

Ever feel like your head is overflowing with tasks, ideas, or emotions? You get in the car and that voice in the back of your mind asks: Did I lock the door? Did I turn off the stove? Are my meeting notes in my bag?

As long as you do nothing with those thoughts, they keep coming back. That creates restlessness and stress. David Allen's method helps you find calm again. It is called a *mind sweep*, or as we like to say, a thought broom.

The process is simple: Clear your head by writing down everything that comes to mind. You can do this on paper or digitally. Take at least half an hour the first time. You will be surprised how clear your mind feels afterward.

The only rule: Do not decide whether something is worth writing down. Just write. When you start looking around and feel more relaxed and notice your head is quiet, you are done. Now you have a clear view of what has been spinning around in your mind.

If you mind sweep regularly, it takes less time. And no, it is not a waste of time. It actually helps you focus on what truly matters. Doing a quick sweep each morning, then updating your to-do list, is a great way to get into gear for the day.

There are other tricks to get things off your mind. One of our colleagues does the grocery shopping during her lunch break. To avoid forgetting the groceries after work, she puts her car keys in the fridge. That way, she does not have to think about it again. Others place a bag by the door or stick a Post-it on it.

Mark uses the mind sweep reactively. "When my head is full of tasks, emotions, or worry, it feels like a train going in circles. By doing a mind sweep, I pull the brakes. It is so ingrained in my life now. Just like brushing my teeth twice a day, this has become a habit too. Simple and reliable. I use it not just to focus at work, but also to fall asleep with a quieter mind."

USE ONE SYSTEM YOU CAN TRUST

Emptying your mind is one thing, but where you empty its contents can make quite a difference. Imagine that in addition to your calendar on your computer, you have a calendar on your phone that doesn't sync with your computer, and you have a paper calendar. If I ask if you can meet for coffee at 4 p.m. next Wednesday, you'd have to check all three calendars to see if you're free. It's an unusual example, of course, but this is exactly what happens when you keep track of your to-dos in multiple places. You might have tasks in your inbox, some notes on your phone to remind you of things you don't want to forget, and maybe even a to-do list on your computer, too. This makes it difficult to stay on top of things and set priorities. Tracking tasks in several different places is technically the same as having no to-do list at all. The trick is to use a single system for all your tasks and projects. If you don't have one system that you can trust completely, your brain will rely on itself to remember tasks anyway, no matter how many times you write something down.

CATCHING INSPIRATION

In addition to tasks, new ideas pop up in our minds willy-nilly. You can't schedule inspiration. It always strikes at random (and often inconvenient) moments: in the shower, while biking, during a walk, in the middle of a meeting. The question is what to do with these thoughts. To avoid forgetting an idea, you have to put in a disproportionate amount of effort to remember it. As a result, you're left with less attention for what you're doing.

Alternatively, if you don't make an effort to retain the idea, there's a good chance you'll forget it. Both options can be stressful. Immediately emptying your mind by writing down your newfound inspiration creates calm and clarity. You can let it go, and have another look at it at a later date.

For example, I used Trello constantly while writing this book. Every time I had an idea for a topic, theme, or sentence, I got it out of my head almost immediately.

> **TEXT YOURSELF TO CLEAR YOUR HEAD**
>
> WhatsApp has embraced the idea of cognitive off-loading by adding a feature that lets you message yourself—a simple way to get things out of your head. Here's how it works:
>
> **Step 1: Start a New Chat**
> Create a new conversation and add yourself as the contact.
>
> **Step 2: Pin the Chat**
> On iPhone: Swipe the chat to the right, then tap pin. On Android: Select the chat, then tap the pin icon. Now the chat will stay at the top for easy access.
>
> **Step 3: Clear Your Head**
> Use it to jot down anything you don't want to forget.

We are big fans of David Allen's GTD method. Here's how we use it to keep as little in our heads as possible.

1. Trello Capture Widget

Whenever someone asks us to do something or we realize we need to do something, we immediately dictate it into our phones. We use the Trello widget for this. With one press of a button, everything is added to our task system (step 2). We also make extensive use of the iPhone's "speech-to-text" feature, which automatically converts everything we say into text.

2. Trello

This is where all our tasks and projects, both work and personal, are listed. Everything is detailed here: we know the underlying objectives and what the next actions are. It works well for us to start each task with a verb. For instance, "Mom's birthday" is too vague; better would be "call brother for Mom's birthday guest list." For each project we are involved in, we have a separate task list.

3. Weekly Review

Once a week, we go through all our tasks and projects. The main goal here is to check if everything is still up-to-date and to determine the focus for the following week.

CLOSING EMOTIONAL LOOPS

The same principle also applies to emotional stuff: things we're worried, angry, or annoyed about. Unlike tasks, these feelings just can't be ticked off, which means they get stuck in our heads. For example, thoughts about uncomfortable conversations we had in the past often spring to mind without warning. Our doubts about them cause us to worry, which saps our energy and makes us more sensitive to distractions. Fortunately, there's something we can do about it.

The best method for this is called *expressive writing*. It's a technique developed by James W. Pennebaker, a professor of psychology at the University of Texas at Austin. Pennebaker discovered that writing down your emotions can lead to significant improvements in both physical and mental health. The beauty of this technique lies in its simplicity: You start by grabbing a pen and paper and finding a quiet place. Then, set a timer for ten to fifteen minutes and write nonstop about whatever comes to mind, without worrying about spelling or grammar. You don't need to keep the text. In fact, you are encouraged to destroy the paper.

It's most effective to repeat this technique for four consecutive days, whenever the need arises. It allows you to get slightly obsessed with the things that bother you. The advice is: "Write and get back to life."

Thousands of studies have been conducted on the benefits of this technique since Pennebaker's initial research. Numerous benefits of expressive writing have been confirmed, including better sleep, reduced stress levels, and a stronger immune system. It even appears to decrease drinking and smoking habits. It's a super simple technique that we recommend to everyone.

> ## ZENPEN.APP
>
> Oscar used expressive writing during a stressful period in his life, which inspired him to create an app for it: Zenpen.app.
>
> It's a chat application, but solely for yourself. Everything you write disappears after thirty seconds. It's made purely for expressing your thoughts. It's completely free and anonymous to use; you don't even need to create an account.
>
> It has helped Oscar tremendously, and he hopes that with this app, more people can benefit from expressive writing.

Another solution: don't fight it. Repressing emotions is like trying to hold an inflatable beach ball underwater; it takes a lot of energy. The harder you try to push it down, the more explosive it is when you let go. This can easily happen when we're tired. Facing your feelings is much more effective. Doing so takes guts and isn't always fun, but it is more productive—personally and professionally.

Finally, it can help to force your mind to analyze situations. The *amygdala*, an area in the middle of our brains, governs our emotions. The more active this part of the brain, the worse your thinking brain performs. You probably know it well: when you're feeling emotional you can't think clearly, no matter if you feel negative or positive emotions. That's why you can be blinded by love or drunk with happiness.

If you're a bit nervous about saying something during an important meeting, it can work wonders to describe the situation or environment in your mind. How many chairs can you see? What colors do you see? What sounds can you hear? Doing this for a few

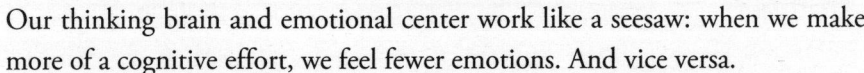

Thinking brain   **Amygdala**

Our thinking brain and emotional center work like a seesaw: when we make more of a cognitive effort, we feel fewer emotions. And vice versa.

seconds will make your amygdala less active, which, in practice, means you won't feel as nervous.

TIMERS AND CHECKLISTS

Another way to employ cognitive distribution is to increase the number of external hard drives you have at your disposal. For example, I make heavy use of the timer on my phone. If I know I have to go out for a meeting fifty minutes from now, I don't want to have to think about it again; I set a forty-five-minute timer, then forget about it. You may think I'm exaggerating, but I've noticed that I think more clearly and experience greater peace of mind when I set a timer well in advance.

Reusable checklists are also effective. I prefer to think about everything once. Thinking about the same exact thing a month later just to come to the same exact conclusion is a huge waste of time. I have checklists for keynotes I give, for everything I have to pack when I travel, and for new product launches. Thanks to these checklists, I don't have to think as much while enjoying the certainty that I won't forget anything. Calm.

GIVE YOUR THINKING BRAIN A BREAK FROM DECISION MAKING

We tend to think mostly in our minds. As a result, our analytical skills are linked to the capacity of our thinking brains. That has its drawbacks at times.

I noticed this the other day when I went to order a new bicycle online. After years of riding around Amsterdam on a rickety old bike, I had decided the time had finally come to replace it with a proper city bike (prompted by the subtle hints my colleagues kept giving me). That's when the fun really started. What brand? What model? What color frame? What color tires? How big a frame should I buy? With or without a crate? What size crate? It wasn't long before I was exhausted.

The more variables involved, the more difficult it gets to maintain clarity. One solution is to sleep on it and let your unconscious mind tackle the problem. This part of our brains has much more thinking power, so it can often come up with an answer by the next morning.[6]

Another option is to use cognitive distribution. In this case, that means using pen and paper to help us make decisions or solve problems whenever possible. The more you manage to empty your mind of all the variables, the more mental space you create to analyze them and the smarter you'll be. You'll be able to use more of your intelligence to make your decision.

FIGHT DECISION FATIGUE WITH ROUTINE

Have you ever noticed how people—okay, mainly men—have the tendency to stand still if you ask them a question while they're walking? I've always found this hilarious, especially since I often catch myself doing this. Essentially, it's a temporary brain overload that causes us to come to a screeching halt. The more you need to think about a question, the less brainpower you have left for basic functions like walking.*

Thinking takes physical effort. If we continue to think for too long we get tired and lose the ability to think clearly. That's why we can make only a limited number of conscious decisions per day, for example. The more decisions we make, the less able we are to make good decisions. This phenomenon is known as *decision fatigue*; it's the reason supermarkets sell candy bars at the checkout counters. By the time we've successfully decided whether we want low-fat or full-fat yogurt, if we want to have rice or pasta tonight, and which of the twenty different pasta sauces is best, our brains will be exhausted and less able to resist a little sugary temptation.

That's why many successful people have made a habit of putting some basic decisions on autopilot so they don't have to think about them anymore. Steve Jobs often wore the same sweater and jeans combo daily, and Barack Obama is known to have the same breakfast every morning. There's logic to this. Mark Zuckerberg, the cofounder of Facebook, who doesn't have a very versatile

---

* It's also the cause of rubbernecking and the resulting traffic jams: We're so curious to find out what happened, we can't resist sneaking a peek. Our brains then have to process what we see, causing us to slow down for a second.

Mark Zuckerberg's wardrobe.⁷

wardrobe either, explained, "I really want to clear my life to make it so that I have to make as few decisions as possible about anything except how to best serve Facebook. I feel like I'm not doing my job if I spend any of my energy on things that are silly or frivolous about my life."⁸

From the brain's perspective, it's wise to spend as little time as possible thinking about everyday matters. The more we think about the little things, the less thinking power we have left for the big picture. That's why routines work so well: they give our minds a well-deserved break. It's a form of cognitive distribution: instead of activating the front of our brains, recurring actions are managed by the back of the brain. This area is mainly made up of basal ganglia cells, which activate when we repeat a task for the third time, allowing us to perform that task without devoting as much targeted attention to it. That's why we can easily talk to people while we're tying our shoes: our basal ganglia cells take over the task of tying laces, freeing up plenty of space for our conversations. It's also how experienced drummers can tap different rhythms with each of their four limbs.

ESTABLISH A MORNING RITUAL

I have a lot of routines, and I've noticed that a fixed morning ritual is especially useful. When I wake up, I take a cold shower, get dressed, meditate for five minutes, drink some lemon juice, have breakfast, then head out to work. All of my working days start the same way. I usually decide what I'm going to wear the evening before, and I rotate between three simple breakfasts. Day 1: low-fat yogurt with muesli. Day 2: vegetable omelet. Day 3: green smoothie.[9] If I had a green smoothie yesterday, I know the low-fat yogurt with muesli is up today. Simplicity: I love it. It lets me focus my attention on the things that matter, like writing this book, without having to think about trivialities too much.

I try to run much of my life on autopilot where possible. I have lunch at a fixed time, I automatically save the same amount of money every month, I always go to the gym on the same days, I listen to the same playlist on Spotify when I want to focus, and I read my email at fixed times.

Though I might seem like a highly structured person, my friends will be quick to tell you I'm the total opposite by nature. I can be quite chaotic at times, but I've noticed that my routines help me master my chaos. The less I have to think about things, the more likely I am to actually do them. It's a much more relaxed approach. Thinking is just like time: it's a limited resource, and you can spend it only once. Be selective.

CALM, CLARITY, AND CONTROL

I recently got an email from the woman I met in Curaçao, telling me she was doing a lot better. She now works with a single, clear list of tasks and projects, always carries a little notebook with her to empty her mind, and goes home at a normal time. "It's not that I've stopped checking my email after 6 p.m., but I definitely think less about work in the evening. There's way less on my mind than before. I sleep better, and I've stopped crashing into desks all the time."

PRACTICAL TIPS TO DECLUTTER YOUR MIND

Tip 1: Fall Asleep Faster with a Mind Sweep
- ✓ Emptying your mind can help you fall asleep. When I still have tasks on my mind late at night, I write them all down on a sticky note to think about later.[10] Basically, it's a rough to-do list. Clearing your mind helps you let go of thoughts, making it easier to drift off to sleep.

Tip 2: Worry Less with 15-Minute Worrying Sessions
- ✓ If you're perpetually haunted by bad memories or doubts, you should probably clear them from your mind. Write down all that ails you on scrap paper, or make a note in your phone, whatever is easiest. Here's how: Write down (1) things you're unsure of or annoyed by and (2) those you need to accept and those you can still change. Finally, (3) do something positive to improve your mood, like making a good cup of coffee or listening to your favorite playlist.

Tip 3: Experiment with Capturing Tasks and Ideas
- ✓ Getting new tasks or ideas out of your head as quickly as possible is a great habit. Use pen and paper or an app; what's important is that you choose one specific way and collect everything in the same place. The goal is to make emptying your mind an automatic behavior. Combining this with Tip 1 will bring you tremendous peace of mind.

CONCENTRATION LEAK 3

Too Little Fuel

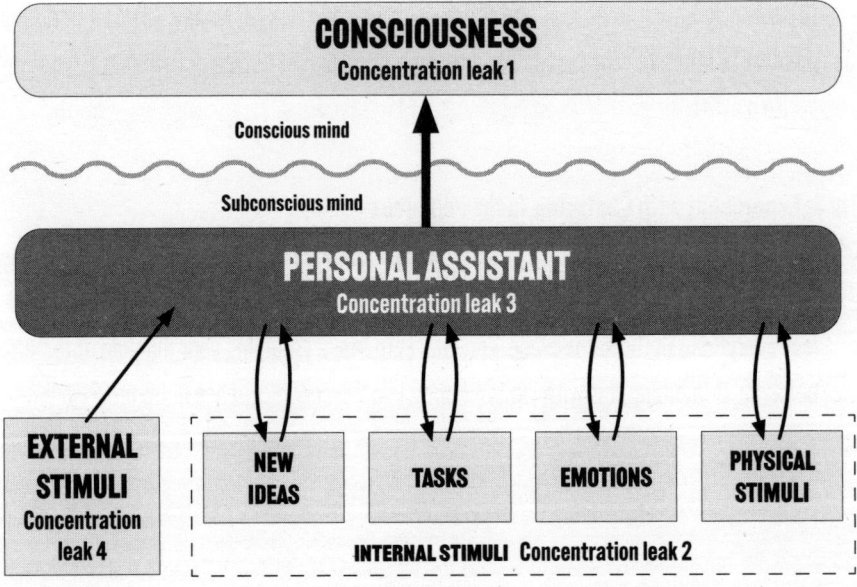

The time you lose by taking a break is smaller than the productivity you lose by pushing through.

FOCUS CHALLENGE

Burnout

A friend of mine works at a law firm where, as in many fields these days, there's a culture of working long hours. In the run-up to important cases everyone stays late—sometimes even sleeping at the office—and coming to work on weekends is pretty standard.

It's appealing in a way: everyone putting in extra hours together, rushing to meet deadlines. It's like a competition of sorts that forces you to push yourself to your limits. But then the extra hours you put in should make sense. And my friend noticed that it was precisely those long days that seriously undermined productivity. "It's all about lasting the longest to showcase your commitment. There's this perception that the people who work the longest also work the hardest, but I tend to do the same amount of work between 4 p.m. and 11 p.m. as I do in the first two hours of the day. Besides, there's also the drawback that structurally working long hours leaves me exhausted. It's a big blow to my productivity; there are days when I get literally nothing done," he confessed.

THERE'S NO LINEAR CORRELATION BETWEEN TIME AND PRODUCTIVITY

We tend to think that the more time we spend on something, the more we get done. It seems straightforward: if you work eight hours you should get twice as much done as you would if you worked four hours, right? Although this can be the case with physical labor, it definitely doesn't apply to brainwork. In the brain, there's no linear correlation between productivity and time. A two-hour meeting doesn't necessarily mean double the productivity of a one-hour meeting. If I were to write for six hours a day I certainly wouldn't write twice as much as I can in three hours.

"In fact, whenever I write more than four hours a day, I find it has a negative impact on my work," Mark Manson, author of the immensely popular book *The Subtle Art of Not Giving a F*ck*, writes on his blog. "In my first year of writing, I still had the mindset that more was better. On my most productive days, I'd write more than 8,000 words in six hours' time. Holy shit! If I continued like this, I'd only need 10 days to finish an entire book! There was only one problem: It all sucked. All of it. When I got to editing later, it turned out that I could only really use 500 of those 8,000 words. The problem was that it would take me four days to pick through the scraps, make some necessary changes, and take out the usable passages. My 'ultra-productive' days put so much extra work on my plate that I'd have been better off if

I hadn't written the 8,000 words in the first place. Even playing video games would've been a better use of my time."[1]

THE BIOLOGY OF ATTENTION

Much of our quality of work and productivity depends on our focus. But just as focus is a limited resource that decreases over time, so is our productivity.

Our personal assistant needs the neurotransmitters noradrenaline and acetylcholine in order to concentrate.[2] They're the fuel for our focus. While noradrenaline focuses our attention on what we're doing, acetylcholine blocks distracting stimuli. At some point, these chemicals run out and you can kiss your focus and productivity goodbye.

If you continue working despite early signs of fatigue, you'll

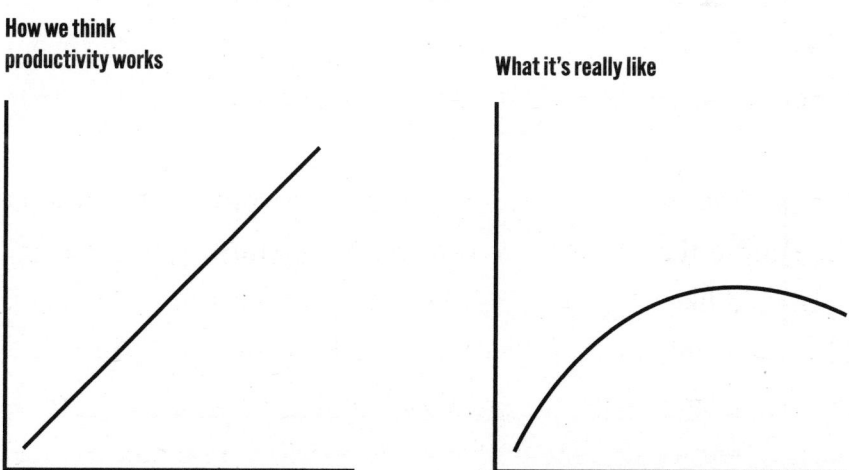

We often imagine that there's a direct, linear relationship between our productivity and the number of hours we spend on a task. In reality, there's a tipping point: at some point, putting in more hours reduces productivity.

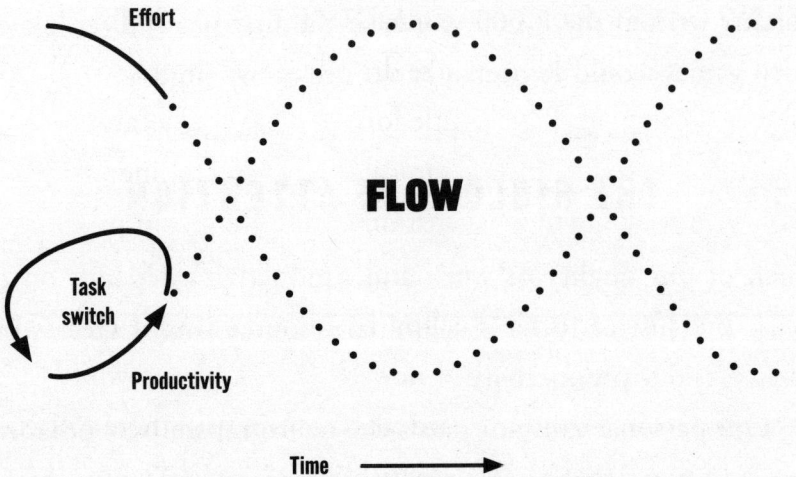

As time passes, your concentration and productivity decline and fatigue increases. At some point, the effort you put into work is not worth what you get out of it. This applies both to blocks of time and to the total number of hours you spend working in a day. When working in blocks, you'll pay the price in the next block. If you work too many hours, you'll pay the price the next day.

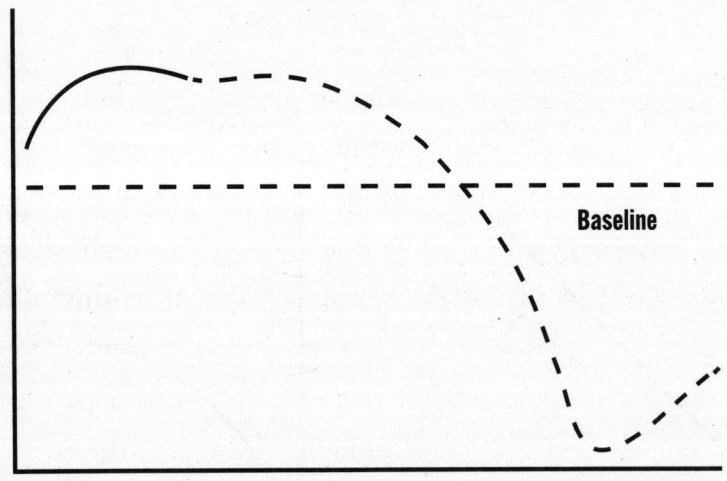

If you continue to work while your brain needs a break, you'll dip into your noradrenaline and acetylcholine reserves. As a result, you won't have enough of these concentration chemicals available the next time you need them, which can lead to deep productivity slumps.

have to tap into your noradrenaline and acetylcholine reserves. Neurologically speaking, you're drawing from your savings: you'll be able to keep working a little longer now, but because you borrowed productivity, your chemical levels will decline. This is the main reason for mental exhaustion and deep dips in productivity. In technical terms, you could compare it to taking MDMA: when it starts to kick in you feel happy, but after you come down you're often left depressed. The bad news is that it takes a while for the body to replenish these chemicals. Fortunately, there are things you can do to avoid productivity dips and make your work less exhausting.

RECHARGE BEFORE YOU GET GOING

The answer to getting more done and experiencing fewer productivity slumps is easy: recharge regularly. It's not so different from bringing an electronic vehicle to a charging station.

The tricky part is that taking a break can feel like a waste of time, especially if you have a lot to do. On busy days, I also have the tendency to keep on working. I want to spend every second I've got on ticking off yet more tasks. Funnily enough, this ultra-productive urge is exactly the reason why I'm ultra-unproductive at times.

I see it in people around me, too. Recently, a partner at a consulting firm told me that "plowing through is the norm, and breaks are for sissies," though he phrased it slightly differently. He works about eighty hours a week and expects his colleagues to do the same. He believed breaks were a waste of time, often had lunch during meetings, and, as he put it, "I don't even go to the bathroom without my phone," his smile betraying his pride in being so busy. Don't get me wrong; I play the same game of maximizing productivity. I just don't think keeping your foot on the gas without stopping to refuel is the best strategy.

How often should we take a break? That depends on the task. When dealing with simple bulk tasks, such as getting rid of a batch of emails, we're most effective when we take a short five-minute break after every twenty-five minutes of work.[3] It might sound like a lot, but speaking from experience I assure you that it's a perfectly pleasant way to work. It's a method known as the *Pomodoro Technique* and it's deservedly famous among productivity experts. The short breaks keep you sharp so you can get more done in a day.

As tasks become more complicated, the Pomodoro Technique becomes less suitable. When tackling more complex issues, we're most effective when we work in blocks of ninety minutes, followed by a fifteen-minute break. Examples include writing a complicated memo or reading an elaborate report. This principle is applied religiously in Finland, where pupils and teachers have a twenty-minute break after every class, with phenomenal results. This may sound strange, but their educational system is considered to be the most effective in the world.

It's certainly possible to spend more than ninety minutes working on a task without taking a break, but, strictly speaking, this doesn't fall into the realm of productivity. We usually use longer blocks to solve problems or create something new, such as writing long articles. This is where productivity evolves into creativity. More on that later.

WATCHING YOUTUBE IS HARD WORK FOR OUR BRAINS

In addition to how many breaks we take, what we do during our breaks determines whether we're recharging or just wasting more energy. In the past, when my energy levels dipped, I stayed behind my computer to watch YouTube videos or scroll through my social media feed. Finally, some me time! Yet after I returned to work, I was often even slower than before the break, getting even less done. But how? After all, I'd just taken a break. Then I learned there are two types of attention: targeted and open attention.

Targeted attention is what you're using now: you're reading the book and absorbing new information. You're having fun—I hope—but it also requires a certain amount of effort, and you won't be able to keep going indefinitely. At some point, you'll need to take a break. Open attention is the total opposite. You're not absorbing new information; you're processing information you already absorbed. It's like daydreaming or spacing out. And it's quite healthy because it activates an area in the brain called the default mode network (DMN).

Because open attention requires a lot less energy than targeted attention, people used to think the DMN was an unimportant area in our brains. Hence its nickname: Does Mostly Nothing.

Today we know this area plays an important role in recharging the brain so you can put your pedal to the metal later on.[4] It's similar to giving your muscles a break after exercising. You'd never work out for eight hours a day without any rest; it's no different for your brain.

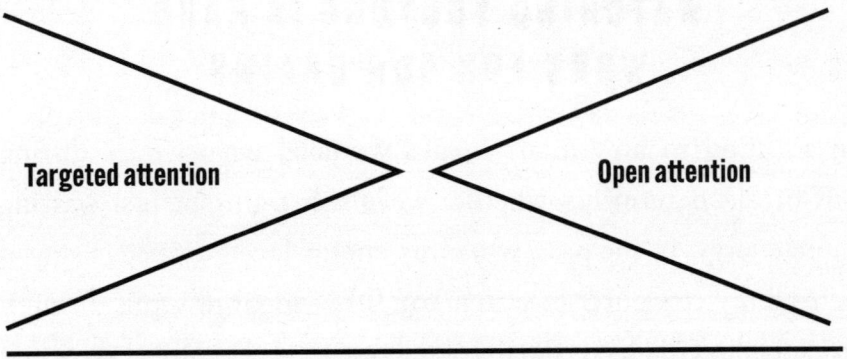

Our attention is like a spectrum, with targeted attention (effort) on one side and open attention (relaxation) on the other.

Now here's the thing: If you watch YouTube or scroll through your phone during your break, you're still absorbing new information. It's probably more fun than Excel spreadsheets, but it still counts as targeted attention. Technically, you're not giving your brain a break at all; it's still hard at work. The tricky part is that you don't feel it, because reading new messages releases happy chemicals, which make you feel as if what you're doing is relaxing when you're actually tiring out your brain even more. "This is exactly why I was always so tired and irritated when I came home from school," Stephanie told me during one of our coaching sessions. She's one of a growing number of teenagers suffering from burnout. She comes from a supportive family, does well in school, and has a good group of friends, but here's her challenge: she gets six hundred WhatsApp messages a day. She likes getting them, but they also exhaust her brain to the point that it burns out.

In my experience, people don't go home tired because of how difficult their days were, but because they didn't recharge their brains enough. The main reason this happens is that we tend to judge the quality of a break by how much we enjoyed it. We think the more fun it is, the more it'll leave us feeling refreshed and recharged. But that's just not how the brain works. Every time it absorbs information it has to work, no matter how much you like the topic. It's better to ask yourself this question: Am I absorbing information? If you are, your brain's at work. If you're not, congratulations, you've just met the first condition for a real break. The second condition? Wandering. We often see daydreaming and drifting off as bad habits to avoid at all costs. However, you can't truly focus until you're also capable of defocusing. The trick is to learn how to deliberately switch between these two types of attention. In fact, that's the main reason why we called this book *Focus ON-OFF*.

Do you ever listen to podcasts? They're entertaining, sure, but they're not breaks. Lounging on the couch with your phone? That's work.

Talking to a colleague? Depends on the topic and on the colleague. Working on a relaxing puzzle? If it's not on your phone, excellent.

Driving? Nope, work.

Staring out the window? Perfect break.

Yoga? Definitely good for your mind and body, but focusing on a pose requires concentration, so it doesn't count as a break. Your thoughts can't wander off. The same goes for intense exercise: you still have to focus. Yoga and exercise aren't enough to recharge your brain, though they're essential to support your mental and physical health and, therefore, your long-term ability to focus and recharge.

> Our main problem these days is not that we have too much stress. It's that we don't recharge our brains.

The best break? Relaxed exercise. Go for a walk. Go grab a cup of coffee somewhere outside the office or on another floor and be sure to take the stairs. Alternating brainwork with physical exertion is a winning combination. For instance, I keep a mini-trampoline next to my desk. Ceiling height permitting, this is a super effective way to recharge: five minutes of jumping is all it takes to get you fully reenergized.

EMBRACE INACTIVITY

In addition to proper breaks, there are moments of boredom: time you spend waiting for people, traveling, waiting in line, and so on. Whenever we're bored we rush to fill our mental void, often grabbing our phones to check Facebook, email, or other social media. I get it. It seems more useful than doing nothing. But boredom is important because it allows our brains to gain new insights and recharge a little. Boredom activates our default mode network, creating precious fuel for later on.

We see being busy as the key to success and the gateway to happiness, but it's good to realize that doing absolutely nothing can sometimes be the most productive option. It's impossible to run at full speed all day long. Personally, I prefer being a bit less sharp while waiting somewhere than feeling dull when I'm at work.

FOCUS BITE

THE BENEFITS OF DOING NOTHING

When you're bored, your brain activates the default mode network. That is when your mind starts tidying up. New experiences get linked to memories, patterns are formed, and things start to make sense. This creates space for creativity and for new ideas to come in. This wandering mode kicks in when you are at rest or not fully focused on a task. That is why the best ideas often pop up at random or inconvenient times: in the shower, on the toilet, in the train, while walking or biking.

We rarely feel bored, but we do nothing quite often. It is basically the same, just with a different label. When you embrace doing nothing, you stop being annoyed by the emptiness of the moment. Finally, nothing on your mind. That is when the default mode network gets going, and new ideas start flowing. In a world full of constant stimuli, doing nothing has become a luxury.

WORK FEWER HOURS

The number of hours we spend working in a day also determines whether we experience productivity slumps. Here's a situation you're probably familiar with: to rush to meet a deadline, you stay late and manage to get your work done. Great, you made it! But the next day you feel like a zombie and end up barely doing anything. Even more frustrating: when you add up all the work you did over the last two days, you realize you did less than if you'd just gone home at a normal time. Sometimes we have to work overtime. It's inevitable, and there's nothing wrong with that. The problems start when it becomes a recurring event. You can't keep a bow drawn forever. The more long hours we work, the less we get done in the long run.

> ## An eighty-hour workweek is not a sign of commitment or dedication; it's a sign of inefficiency.

This was confirmed in a study by Stanford University researchers who gave their test subjects a week to work their way through a lengthy list of tasks.[5] The subjects were divided into two groups: the first had forty hours to work on the to-do list, while the others were given sixty hours for the same list. When the researchers looked at which group had checked off the most tasks on Monday, they weren't surprised to find the sixty-hour group had completed more tasks. After all, when the other group headed home the first day at 5 p.m., they kept their heads down and got back to work. However, the group working longer hours was a little more tired when they came in the next day, hurting

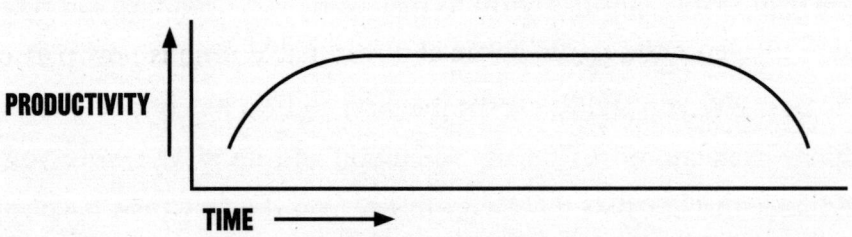

When you work long hours or do so too often, you get less done than if you were to go home at a normal time.

their productivity. The same thing happened on day two. As mental fatigue increased, their productivity slumped. By the end of the week, the group working sixty hours was about 30 percent less productive than the group working only forty hours. Bizarre, right? When we work less, we get more done. Conclusion: regular overtime is a bad idea.*

But the times, they are a-changin'. More and more people are sick and tired of constantly being at work. Guilt about never seeing children and significant others, perpetual tiredness, stress, and trouble falling asleep are common symptoms. We're all fed up.

The thing is, you can't just tell people to stop checking work email in the evening. It's too addictive. No one wants to be that person who didn't read the important email in time. That's why Volkswagen and BMW decided to adjust their servers to stop sending emails after 7 p.m. If there's no email traffic, there's nothing to check. Sure, you can send emails, but they won't arrive until the next morning. Now their employees can rest assured that they won't miss a thing when they go home and enjoy a quiet evening.

France took matters a step further. The country passed laws to stop managers from contacting employees on days off. It's even punishable by law to ask employees questions when they're not at work.[6]

In Denmark, going home at a reasonable time is now part of the culture. Working overtime is a thing of the past. At the vast majority of companies, everyone—from juniors to seniors—clocks in at 9 a.m. and heads home at 5 p.m. In fact, failing to do so will get

---

* Ironically, I'm writing this at 11:42 p.m. after a fourteen-hour working day. Note to self: stop writing.

you raised eyebrows about your effectiveness. Clearly it's working: Denmark is the happiest country in the world and one of the most productive countries in the EU. Helen Russell, a British author who moved to Denmark when her husband got a job there, puts it nicely: "I thought they were lazy at first, but they're just focused. They don't check their Facebook profile every thirty minutes when they're at work. There's a strict separation between work and time off, and that's a good thing: it gives us more peace of mind and reduces the risk of burnouts."[7]

It's a hot topic in Sweden, too, where several organizations have adopted six-hour workdays while still paying their employees for eight hours. This approach is paying off well for the companies that could afford to do so: sickness absenteeism has plunged, employees are happier, and productivity has skyrocketed.

Countries like Spain, Belgium, Portugal, and Italy have now introduced similar right-to-disconnect laws. Unfortunately, the Netherlands has not followed suit yet, despite several initiatives. It's a missed opportunity, because laws like these could really ease the pressure to always be available.

"We thought trimming the workweek would force us to hire more people, but the efficiency gains mean the current workforce will do just fine," says Maria Bråth, who runs a search optimization company. Since the company introduced a thirty-hour workweek it has seen its revenue double every year for three years.[8]

More and more scientific studies are showing that eight-hour workdays are inefficient. Sure, we can perform eight hours of physical labor a day, but when it comes to knowledge work, we should consider ourselves lucky if we can concentrate for four hours a day.[9]

POOR SLEEP CAN COST YOU
$1,967 USD PER YEAR

Sleep is the ultimate break, and our brains need it desperately in order to function properly. After being awake and alert for hours, the brain needs to recover.

The areas of our brains that were active during the day become active once more during REM sleep—reliving the day, you could say. This helps the brain consolidate important information and get rid of redundant data. When we don't sleep long enough we disrupt this process and our cognitive performance deteriorates.[10]

Not sleeping enough causes our IQs to drop by about ten points, which makes us slower, less alert, and more prone to error. It's important to note that this happens even if you don't miss a full night of sleep: even losing out on a few hours of sleep, or not sleeping soundly, negatively affects your brain. Reduced productivity caused by poor sleep costs society an average of $1,967 per person, per year.[11]

> After not sleeping for twenty-one hours, you have the same cognitive ability as you do when you're drunk.

When we don't get enough sleep, we're much more emotional and sensitive to negative emotions the next day—hardly beneficial for our performance.[12] That's because our amygdala (which regulates emotions, remember?) and our prefrontal cortex (which normally calms things down) aren't functioning as they should.[13]

"Sleep is a prerequisite for excellent performance. It's even more important than a healthy diet and exercise put together," sleep expert Floris Wouterson told me in one of our interviews. "Time and time again, I find that people overestimate how well they can cope with little sleep. We may think that our performance doesn't suffer from minor sleep deprivation, but it does."

Wouterson is referring to a well-known study on the relationship between sleep deprivation and performance. The subjects were allowed to sleep four, six, or eight hours a night for two weeks, and one particularly unfortunate participant was kept awake for three days straight.[14]

Next, the researchers examined who performed best with various tasks. Unsurprisingly, the group getting eight hours of sleep came first. What you might not have expected is that though the groups sleeping four and six hours a night thought they performed okay, their scores were actually just as bad as the person who stayed up for three days straight.[15]

The outcome of the study: sleeping fewer than six hours is just as detrimental to your productivity as not sleeping at all. That's why I'm not a big fan of productivity gurus who recommend getting up at 5 a.m. to reach peak productivity. It's possible, sure, but only if you go to bed no later than 9 p.m.

SLEEP: QUALITY OVER QUANTITY

How much sleep we get is an important factor, but the quality of sleep also plays an important role. When it comes to feeling relaxed and reenergized, quality comes first.[16] Here are some practical tips to improve the quality of your sleep.

Establish a Fixed Rhythm

People with irregular sleeping patterns don't sleep as deeply as people with fixed sleep schedules. That's not just because they go to bed at different times, but also because their evening rhythms change when they come home later. If possible, make sure to go home at a regular time, follow a fixed evening routine, and go to bed and wake up at the same time each day.

Find Yourself a Quiet, Dark Place to Sleep

At night we go through several phases of sleep, each of which has its own function. One of these phases is deep sleep, when the brain tidies up. All the important information it absorbed that day is archived and any unnecessary scraps are thrown out, creating space.

This process is very sensitive to light and sound, which can mess up the consolidation process even if they don't wake you up. Make sure you sleep in a silent, pitch-black room.

For that reason, a renowned international soccer club tapes off all light sources in the players' hotel rooms before game day. Black stickers cover TV standby buttons, extra layers of cloth are used to darken the curtains, and thick doormats stop outside light from creeping in. This improves the players' deep sleep phase and boosts their performance. It seems sleeping masks aren't so silly after all!

Buy a Wake-Up Light

Have you ever gotten eight hours of sleep, only to wake up feeling as if you haven't slept a wink? Chances are your alarm went off while you were still in your deep sleep phase. That's the big drawback of traditional alarm clocks: they don't care about our sleep rhythms. Wake-up lights, on the other hand, do. Half an hour before you want to wake up they start emitting a soft light which stops your body from producing melatonin, a sleep hormone that causes you to fall and stay asleep. You'll wake up more naturally as a result. Highly recommended.

Power Nap

If you find you're a bit tired in the afternoon but still have some work to do, taking a nap is a perfect way to recharge your batteries. It's better than caffeine, and it'll even keep you feeling energized longer.

How long should you nap? That depends on your goal. If you're looking for a fresh dose of energy and alertness, all it takes is ten minutes. If you still have some heavy cognitive lifting ahead of you in the evening, or if you want to stay sharp during a business dinner, getting at least ninety minutes of midday shut-eye can help.

Elite athletes and NASA pilots swear by it, and it's becoming more and more of an accepted practice in businesses. Google's offices, for example, feature dedicated rooms where employees can take a nap. It's simple arithmetic: the time they spend sleeping is balanced out by increased productivity and reduced sick days taken.

A quick note: Avoid sleeping between forty-five and ninety minutes. That is when you are likely to be in the middle of a deep sleep cycle. If you wake up during that phase, you can experience sleep inertia. You will feel groggy and disoriented for a while.

FOCUS BITE

DOES SLEEP MAKE YOU MORE CREATIVE?

Spoiler: it is mostly about waking up at the right moment. That is what surrealist artist Salvador Dalí and famous inventor Thomas Edison did. To boost their creativity, they would fall asleep sitting in a chair while holding something small—like a pen or a paper cup—in their hands. As soon as they nodded off, the object would drop to the floor. The sound woke them up instantly.

That exact moment mattered, because they believed they were in a creative state where reality blends into imagination. This early sleep phase is called the hypnagogic state, or N1 stage, and it lasts only a few minutes.

To see if this works for regular people too, researchers at the Paris Brain Institute ran a study. Participants were asked to solve difficult math problems without knowing there was a hidden pattern. Spotting the pattern made the task much easier.

Each sleep stage creates a different brain wave pattern, so the researchers used EEG to track when participants shifted from N1 to deeper sleep (N2). They discovered that people who spent at least fifteen seconds in the N1 stage had an 83 percent chance of finding the hidden pattern. That dropped to 30 percent for those who stayed fully awake.

As soon as participants slipped into deeper sleep, the effect disappeared.

> That is strong evidence that there is a sweet creative spot just before you fully drift off. In this half-awake state, your brain forms more connections. You are more open to new information and better at seeing patterns you would normally miss.
>
> So next time you get woken up by your kids, the dog, the newspaper, noisy neighbors, a street sweeper, airplanes, or drunk students—try not to sigh. Instead, seize the moment to generate a new idea.

I WORK, THEREFORE I AM

Taking breaks is easier said than done. At least, for me it is. I'm writing this chapter on a family vacation. We're having a great time, but I struggle to resist work's call. I should be doing nothing. Recharging. I know it's important, yet it's still a challenge. I want to keep moving; standing still doesn't satisfy me. If you're positively inclined you could call me "driven," but the reality is less charming: When I'm not working, I don't feel okay. I have to work.

It's a kind of overcompensation I also see in others: "I feel like I'm not good enough, but as long as I put in enough effort and accomplish as much as I can I'll be okay." The permanent sense of unease causes many people to never switch off and struggle to do nothing.

We always want (need?) to grow to the next level. Often we say to ourselves: "All I want to do is reach X. When that happens, I'll have succeeded and I can start relaxing." But it's a mirage: every time you think you've reached the finish line, it moves. It's never good enough.

This is exactly why it's difficult to enjoy doing nothing and living in the present. It's no surprise, since we're constantly rewarded for being productive. Problem is, by doing so we're ignoring the fact that sometimes you have to stand still to move forward. Doing nothing is highly underrated.

We're so addicted to constant progress that we even fill up our time with less important tasks just for the sake of staying busy, also known as busywork.

PING-PONG TABLES

The law firm from the start of this chapter has since banned lunchtime meetings. Instead, the office cafeteria now boasts Ping-Pong and pool tables. It's not the only company in the midst of a change. More and more knowledge-intensive organizations have started offering yoga and sports classes during office hours. While overtime and sleep deprivation used to be viewed as badges of honor, striking the right balance between grinding and recharging is the new cool.

PRACTICAL TIPS TO FUEL YOUR FOCUS AND FEND OFF BURNOUT

Tip 1: Take the Focus OFF Challenge
- ✓ Over the next ten working days, schedule at least one break a day in which you don't absorb any new information and you allow your thoughts to wander. No social media, email, WhatsApp, podcasts, or newspapers. Take a walk, for example, and leave your phone at your desk. Just staring out the window also works; it's something you can easily do every time you have a few minutes to kill before your next meeting or before you go to bed.

Tip 2: Improve Your Sleep Step by Step
- ✓ Systematically improving your sleep has a fantastic effect on your concentration and productivity. Start in your bedroom. Make it as dark and quiet as possible.[17] Make sure it's neat and tidy, and shut it off completely from your work. The goal is for your bedroom to become an oasis of peace. Then adjust your day: stop drinking coffee after 2 p.m. and make sure to get plenty of exercise.[18]

Tip 3: Create a Clear Dividing Line from Work with a Checkout Routine
- ✓ A smidgen of stress isn't necessarily bad for the brain; only constant stress is. Latent stress occurs when we're always busy with work and never really relax. One of the best things you can do is to stop working entirely after the working day is done. No more email, no more work-related messages, no more reading, no more nothing. Zilch. Nada. Niente. A *checkout routine* can be a huge help. Five minutes before you go home, read your email one final time, check tomorrow's calendar, and do one last mind sweep to empty your head. If another task or idea springs to mind, clear it from your mind by writing it down.

CONCENTRATION LEAK 4

Too Many External Stimuli

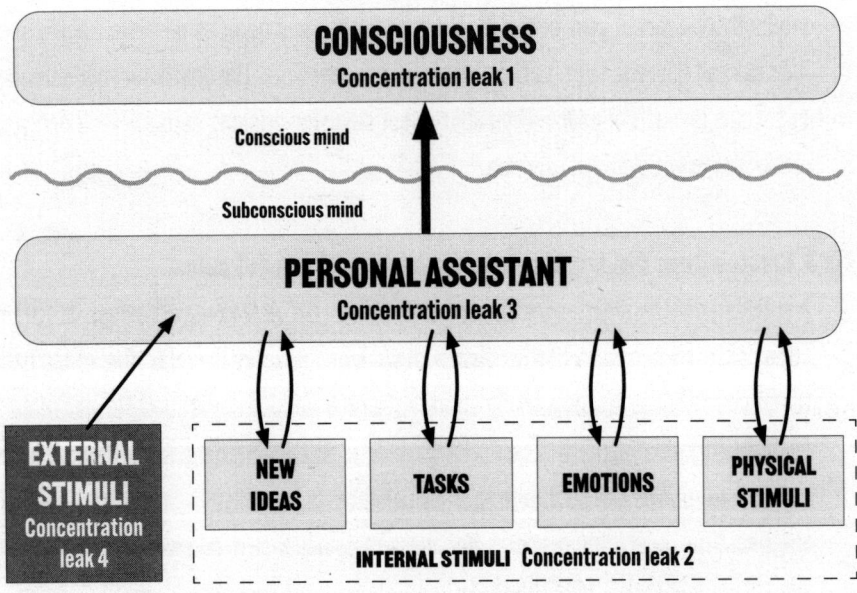

Focus means saying no a thousand times before you say yes.

FOCUS CHALLENGE

Always Available

In high school, I had a classmate named Claire. We hung out together often and always kept in touch. Claire was great with numbers and graciously let me copy many math tests. After graduating, she became an accountant for a large firm, and she worked her way up to partner in the twelve years since. Swelling with pride, she recently told me she now has her own office where she advises clients on tax strategy. Heading a team of junior accountants who mainly handle the operational side of things gives her more time to work on strategies with her clients.

Over the course of the day, she gets about a hundred emails and several phone calls, and her juniors regularly come to her with questions. Her door is always open because she wants to encourage people to ask questions. "After all, part of my role is to help them develop."

At first, she loved how often her team members interrupted

her: it was a sign they needed her and it made her feel important. It also gave her a kind of rush: she had to constantly switch from one topic to the next, resulting in highly dynamic workdays.

The initial enjoyment she got from all those interruptions, however, gradually gave way to the realization that she got none of her own work done. She noticed she had trouble diving deep. Every time she sat down to sink her teeth into an article, she was interrupted and had to readjust. It started sapping her energy while her own work piled up. "I'd become my team's aide rather than their boss, turning my days into mosaics of bits and pieces of other people's work while my own concentration continued to decline. My energy levels bottomed out and I didn't feel like doing anything. Everything just took way too much effort. I'd go home tired and dissatisfied day in and day out," she told me. A few months later, she was diagnosed with burnout.

FRAGMENTED DAYS

Think back to a day when you remember yourself being immensely productive. Maybe you set yourself a clear list of tasks and worked through all of them without disruption. One glorious day when you finally made actual progress on a project that had been on your desk for a while. A day when you went home satisfied and full of energy after work.

It sounds like an ideal day, but for most of us, these days are the exception rather than the rule. We rarely get to choose what we focus our attention on as it's usually determined by the people around us. An incoming email might distract you from the report you intended to write, or a coworker may want to run something by you, all at the expense of your preparations for tomorrow's presentation. Even something as tiny as a text message sent during an important meeting can cause you to miss out on parts of the conversation.

"Stress is always around the corner in this fragmented approach, making it difficult to work effectively," say Jason Fried and David Heinemeier Hansson, who run the successful software company Basecamp together. "Twenty-five minutes on the phone, ten minutes helping a coworker, five minutes for what you should actually be working on before you're sucked into another fifteen-minute conversation that didn't need your attention in the first place. When everything's said and done, you're left with a generous five minutes to do what you had wanted to."[1]

> **We don't have workdays; we have work minutes.**
>
> Gloria Mark, professor of informatics

Our fragmented hours mean we mainly take a reactive approach to work. We become slaves to everything happening around us: busy, but not so productive. This kind of work prevents us from really diving deep. Imagine how weird it would be if a soccer coach substituted his players every five minutes. Why would it be any different for the brain?

Rarely do we immediately resume the tasks we were working on after being interrupted. Often we do another small task in between, which is why it takes an average of twenty-three minutes before we return to the original task.² If the tasks we do in between require our full attention, we might even completely forget about what we were doing first. Have you ever gone to shut down your computer, and then suddenly realized you still have two half-finished emails to write?

WORKING WITHOUT INTERRUPTIONS

Open any biography, and you'll find that virtually every accomplished genius, successful businessperson, or renowned musician regularly retreats from the world to work without disruption. Some go on long walks, others lock themselves into luxury hotel rooms, shut off from phone calls, colleagues, and email. As Picasso's golden rule says: "Without great solitude, no serious work is possible." It's a hint. Isolating yourself gives you the opportunity to tackle a task without interruption, letting you make real progress, dive deep, gain new insights, finish projects, and deliver masterpieces.

"But what if I miss an important message?" It's a common and legitimate question at the very heart of why this is so challenging. We want (need?) to be available at all times and don't want to (can't?) miss a thing. This isn't the weirdest impulse in the world; it lets us stay on the ball and shift gears quickly. It's important, for sure, and it can be enjoyable. But being on the ball all day isn't.

If we don't have stretches of time when we can really work on a task without something else popping up, we'll never make real progress, which can be very frustrating and stressful. I see it happen around me all the time: people on the verge of tears because they can't get anything done unless it's 9 p.m. and they aren't being emailed every other minute. This isn't healthy.

The fact that you feel compelled to be available at all times is a sign that work hasn't been divided properly. Having to keep an eye on your inbox all day long isn't normal; your coworkers shouldn't be allowed to interrupt you all day long. You wouldn't expect a surgeon to keep one eye on the hospital lobby to check for new emergency patients in the middle of a heart operation.

I'm not saying we should work in full focus and complete isolation at all times. Becoming a hermit won't help your reputation in the office, and having customers and colleagues wait ages for answers is a big no-no. In order to fully focus on work more often, we have to rearrange our schedules to free up blocks of time to work without interruptions. Here's how.

LIMIT YOUR NOTIFICATIONS

"What interrupts you at work?" I asked Thomas. He's a Google Ads expert at a New York advertising agency. The company is cool as can be, but its revenue is growing at the same rate as its number of new burnout cases.

"Well, the list goes on," he began. "There are emails and phone calls, of course, but I also get tons of notifications from apps on my phone and computer. We use Skype to chat inside the office, and I get new messages all day. There's a constant flow of WhatsApp messages from friends and coworkers because we have several groups to solve problems quickly, and notifications from Trello, which we use for all our projects."

While he tries to focus on his tasks, he also has to scan five other channels for important messages. "Most of it isn't urgent, but you can't know until after you've checked." By the time you do, your focus has flown out the window.

The problem with our current setup is that urgent messages are sent on the same channels as nonurgent messages. You have to keep an eye on everything for fear of being the focused nerd who misses the critical memo. The first step toward less stress is setting up a single channel for issues that have to be resolved or dealt with immediately. Move all other messages to separate channels and make sure you aren't expected to respond immediately.

It's not something you can do on your own. It requires a culture shift at work. You have to be backed by your organization, which is exactly what Thomas's company decided to do. At first, some people had to be reminded that personal questions about days off weren't exactly urgent, but everyone got into the flow after the first month or two. "We're all more structured and considerably calmer now," Thomas told me, "even though we're busier than ever."

While we're on the subject, let me tell you why I don't believe in turning off all notifications. They can be very useful, but only if we use them selectively. All my WhatsApp notifications, for example, are off, and I check my messages only four or five times a day. People know they can call or text me for urgent matters, and I'll respond immediately. I still don't miss a thing, but I manage to avoid being distracted by fun—though not exactly urgent—cat videos.

My calendar notifications are on so I receive reminders about my meeting with Pete in twenty minutes, for example. It's necessary because without this reminder I would have been late.

I switched off my email notifications; they're just too generic. Too many emails simply aren't urgent. If I checked every incoming message right away, you wouldn't be reading this book right now.

Don't say, "Ah, but I always ignore my notifications." It's impossible not to pay attention to the pings of incoming messages. Even if you consciously decide to ignore them, you've already lost the battle. Not reading the message requires willpower, which is a limited resource. The more willpower you use by not looking at your phone, the less you have left to resist other temptations like sugary treats. Scientists have even found that we find it more difficult to ignore a notification than to resist a chocolate bar or sex.[3] (I'm curious as to how they tested that, but that's another matter.)

Now I'm not trying to force you to check your inbox only four times a day if it means you'll become a nervous wreck because you're afraid of missing something urgent. That would simply mean replacing an external distractor with an internal one. Then we'd be right back where we started. Set things up so urgent messages come in through a separate channel with active notifications, then try to find a rhythm for checking nonurgent messages. It doesn't really matter how often you do: checking your mail every thirty minutes is a whole lot better than constantly being interrupted by notifications.

THE FOCUS QUADRANT

A good work setup is like deep-sea diving, which is something I love doing. One of the first things you learn is that you shouldn't resurface in one go after a deep dive. Nitrogen bubbles could form in your blood if you do, which isn't very good for you. That's why divers use safety stops: well before you reach the surface, you wait until your body safely releases its nitrogen before you fully resurface.

Underwater, there's a simple rule: the longer and deeper the dive, the more safety stops you need. The deeper you dive, the longer it takes to get back to the surface. There's a clear parallel with work here.

The more complex the task and the more deeply we think about it, the longer it takes us to recover. I've noticed that after writing for a while, I have to wait at least fifteen minutes before I can have a normal conversation again.

I'm sure you know the frustrations of getting a phone call moments after sitting down to work on something complex. Imagine if you were diving and had to resurface every few minutes. You'd be slightly annoyed, to say the least, as it would take ages to finally dive deep.

Translating this analogy to work, you'll find that as tasks get more complex, interruptions become more annoying. If you know you might be interrupted at any time it's better to avoid tasks requiring major cognitive effort. If you don't, you've got yourself a recipe for stress and frustration. When interruptions are likely, it's much healthier to focus on simple tasks and stay closer to the surface where interruptions aren't as severe.

Alternatively, it's a bit of a waste to do simple, superficial tasks when we (finally) have a space to work without interruptions. When you find yourself in that situation, don't be afraid to dive deep. I've found a setup that works wonders: schedule simple tasks when you know you'll be interrupted often, and leave tasks requiring deeper thought for quieter times.

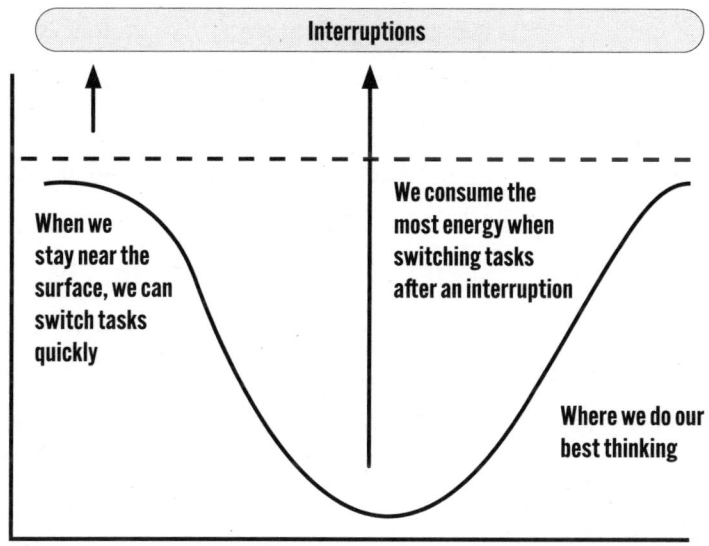

You can compare working to deep-sea diving: the deeper the dive, the longer it takes to resurface. Rushing back to the surface isn't very comfortable.

Think of it as a quadrant. If you know you'll be interrupted often, there's also a greater chance you'll put off complex tasks. In order to avoid alternating deep dives with easy questions, you'll unconsciously start prioritizing simple tasks. We often think we're procrastinating because we're not motivated, but in reality it's our lack of opportunities to work undisturbed. Now let's look at how we can reduce how often we're interrupted.

	SIMPLE TASKS	**COMPLEX TASKS**
Many interruptions	- Only feasible option - Feel well organized - Suffer least from switches	- Frustration and stress - High risk of mistakes - Suffer most from switches
Few interruptions	- Waste - Unsatisfied feeling	- Make real progress - Gives the most satisfaction

USE A SIGNAL

In many hospitals in the Netherlands there's a rule that people administering patients' medications must wear brightly colored vests. This lets everyone know they're not to be disturbed to help avoid potentially fatal mistakes. (It's a bit odd that the doctors who prescribe the medications are constantly interrupted throughout their shifts, but that's another issue altogether.)

I don't know if wearing a neon DO NOT DISTURB vest is quite the solution you were looking for, so here's an alternative: the desktop focus light. It works just like a traffic light—red means don't disturb; green means please come in, ask away, and tell me all about your wonderful weekend.

SCHEDULE MEETINGS WITH YOURSELF

During meetings, we're a lot less likely to be interrupted than when we're sitting at our desks. Use this to your advantage and schedule more of them . . . with yourself. Block off the next hour in your calendar to tell everyone you're unavailable. Set your phone to airplane mode; switch off your email notifications. One task, one application, one goal.

One hour of focus a day keeps the doctor away.

Work somewhere other than your office at least one day a week. This one won't work in all fields, but if it's an option for you, I recommend it. Go somewhere you can work comfortably and make sure no one knows where you are.

FIXED WALK-IN HOURS

I'm not a fan of open-door policies. If they are your cup of tea, why not get rid of personal offices altogether and opt for an open office? The two aren't all that different to your brain. If you do have your own office, use it to your benefit and set fixed walk-in hours. If the building is on fire people are welcome to disturb you, but for everything else they can come in only from 11 a.m. to noon and 3 p.m. to 4 p.m., for example. Setting office hours gives you more control over your own schedule and will help you focus and get more done. Besides, setting limited discussion hours encourages people to work more independently and generally forces them to be better prepared when they do come to see you.

FEWER INTERRUPTIONS, GREATER SATISFACTION

Stress, big workloads, and sick days can largely be explained by the number of times you're interrupted each day. Minimizing interruptions lets you dive deeper, work more comfortably, finish your tasks faster, and go home satisfied more often.

Claire has now returned to work. "Since I started minimizing interruptions and set fixed hours for walk-ins, things are much better. I'm enjoying work again and can finally get things done. Hectic days still sweep me off my feet from time to time, but what I feared most—missing important messages and [having] angry colleagues—has failed to materialize. I don't miss a thing. Oddly enough, my colleagues also prefer this system. I suspect they're secretly a little jealous."

PRACTICAL TIPS TO MANAGE EXTERNAL STIMULI AND REDUCE INTERRUPTIONS

Tip 1: Take the Notification Challenge
- ✓ Here's how it works: For the next seven days, you're going to switch off all notifications except for your SMS and calendar notifications. Grab your mobile phone, go to settings, and tap on "notifications." You'll now see a list of all the apps installed on your phone. Here, you can choose which apps can send notifications. The first three days may be a little uncomfortable, but you'll soon realize that freeing yourself from notifications opens up an oasis of peace.

Tip 2: Set Up an Out-of-Office Message Even Though You're in the Office
- ✓ Several days a week, schedule time to shut yourself off and work on complex tasks requiring a bit more thought. What can really help is setting up an out-of-office message during these dedicated focus time slots, even though you're still there. For example, "Hi, I'm currently working on an important task and won't check my email until noon. For urgent matters, please call me at . . ."

Tip 3: Label Your Tasks
- ✓ Labeling your tasks as simple chores or deep dives can also help. On days with lots of appointments or a high chance of being interrupted, you can get cracking on your list of easy, simple tasks—perfect for hectic, fragmented days. Vice versa, when you know you won't be interrupted for a while, you'll have various complex task suggestions at your fingertips.

FOCUS CHALLENGE

Too Much Noise

"Ever since we moved to our new office, I'm completely exhausted by the time I come home," Alisa tells me. She's the financial director for a well-known clothing brand. "It's weird: my workload hasn't changed at all, but I have to put in a lot more effort to get anything done. Things that I polish off in two hours at home can easily take five hours at the office." The problem? Her new office is open-plan. If you're familiar with working in an open office, you probably know how difficult it can be to fully focus. The noise levels that come with open offices have a particularly significant impact on our productivity.

OPEN-PLAN OFFICES: PROS AND CONS

Now, I'm not one to argue that we should go back to being cubicle-dwelling, box-ticking machines working in complete isolation, but I do think we should take our brains' needs into account when designing a workplace. If you don't, you can still create a cool social hangout space, but don't expect people to work with any kind of efficiency.

And if there's one thing that hinders our brains, it's working together in one open space. Open offices are a product of the 1950s, based on the idea that removing all walls would make it easier to talk with one another, thus increasing company synergy and boosting productivity. The stuff of bosses' dreams. But science and the countless people I've spoken to about the issue prove this isn't quite how it works in the real world.

True, it's a lot easier to talk to others in an open office, but because everyone can listen in there's little privacy. In turn, this means people are less inclined to have in-depth conversations and really open up to one another. Ironically enough, that's why open offices yield less face-to-face contact and a 30 percent increase in digital traffic. Instead of having a chat in the real world, we resort to sending emails or messages.[1]

But there's an even bigger disadvantage to open offices: noise. As you probably know, to say it's distracting is an understatement. Focusing on your work is utterly impossible if you're also listening in on the conversation about next weekend's dinner plans happening next to you. Your brain just wasn't built to do two things consciously at the same time. That's the problem with open offices: we can't switch off our ears. And because most topics for discussion in an office often involve you in some way, every single external stimulus activates the cocktail party effect.

In a study by Alan Hedge, emeritus professor at Cornell University, no fewer than 74 percent of test subjects believed their workplaces were too noisy to be able to concentrate. Between chatting colleagues, symphonies of phone notifications, whining printers, incoming email bells, people pacing during phone calls, and finally, people who receive emails from colleagues and decide to shout their replies across the office, it's amazing we ever get anything done at all. All it takes is one person to distract a whole team or frustrate an entire office.

Noise is one of the most potent factors hurting our productivity, and it costs European businesses some €30.8 million a year. It even undermines our health:[2] people in open-plan offices take 62 percent more sick days.[3] Intellectual work requires quiet surroundings with as little distraction as possible. The harder the task, the more essential quiet is.[4]

AUDITORY DISTRACTION

The reason auditory stimuli are so harmful is that they activate our thinking brains. They're processed by the same area we use to analyze information, taking up valuable cognitive real estate. You won't be as bothered by noise when working through routine chores, but it becomes a real problem when we have to sit down and think. Noise makes it harder to focus on the task at hand.

That colleague having a conversation next to you can cause your productivity to drop by well over 60 percent.[5] If this continues all day long, it means we need to work for an extra ninety minutes just to get everything done.[6] There is, however, a difference between extroverted and introverted people; introverts suffer even more from external noise and stimuli.

30% EXTERNAL STIMULI	70% SPACE FOR THE TASK ITSELF

When part of our minds are occupied by external stimuli, there's less space for the task itself. Because of the reduced availability of brain activity, we have to put in more effort to do the same amount of work.

TAKING CONTROL BY TAKING BREAKS

When we're distracted by noise we tend to turn to our colleagues for the solution ("Shut up, all of you!"), but how easily we get distracted is mostly determined by our own approach to work. More specifically, how we use our thinking brains. Here's how it works: Distracting stimuli are blocked by an area of the brain called the *superior prefrontal cortex*, which is part of our thinking brains. When our minds are full of things to remember, they take up a big chunk of our thinking brains, literally leaving less space for the superior prefrontal cortex to function properly.[7]

The same applies when we work on many different projects simultaneously and switch from one task to another. Every time we switch, our brains temporarily run at half speed, making them less capable of blocking distracting sounds.

Not taking enough breaks can also negatively affect the superior prefrontal cortex. If you want to arm yourself against office noise, make sure to take regular breaks. Doing so will make your brain more resilient to noise.

"Don't forget to get some milk!"	Less space for the superior prefrontal cortex to block stimuli

It's also good to realize that when ambient noise starts bothering you it's actually a sign that the task you're working on is too easy. To really shut yourself off from colleagues passionately recapping last night's basketball game, simply ensure that there's no space left for distractions in your mind. Make the task at hand more challenging by following the "filling the void" principle.

MINIMALISM AND FOCUS

Right now, your eyes are scanning everything around you, whether you're conscious of it or not. It's impossible for your eyes not to see. The more stuff around you, the more your eyes have to scan, and the fuller your thinking brain will be. This is why a messy desk poaches 12 percent of your concentration.[8] An easy way to improve your productivity is to tidy up your desk and empty it completely: minimize to maximize.

Your desk is a microcosm of your office, or even your entire home. The more stuff you own, the more you have to think about. For instance, the documents tucked away in the drawer that you'll deal with eventually, or that box of stuff in the garage you can't bring yourself to throw away just yet. Everything you own, everything you have to do, and everything you have to make a decision about takes up a precious piece of brain capacity. The fewer things you have, the less you'll have on your mind—and your desk—and the more productive (and often happier) you'll be. There is a clear link between focus and minimalism.

ACHIEVING COLLECTIVE QUIET

There's a lot we can do on our own to reduce distractions from noise, but there's still plenty you can do together to make the office a less distracting place.

Have Everyone Turn Off the Peeps 'n' Beeps

This one is easier said than done. To ensure success, start by asking your colleagues how they feel about having to listen to other people's phones. Most people will jump at the chance to complain about how annoying other people's notifications are, presenting you with a nice route to suggesting "notification-free" zones.

From Sound to Silence

Neuropsychiatrist Theo Compernolle has a simple yet effective solution for open offices: create a street leading from sound to silence. When you enter the office, there's a social corner where everyone can chat freely, followed by a section for working on projects together. At the back of the office you'll find the focus

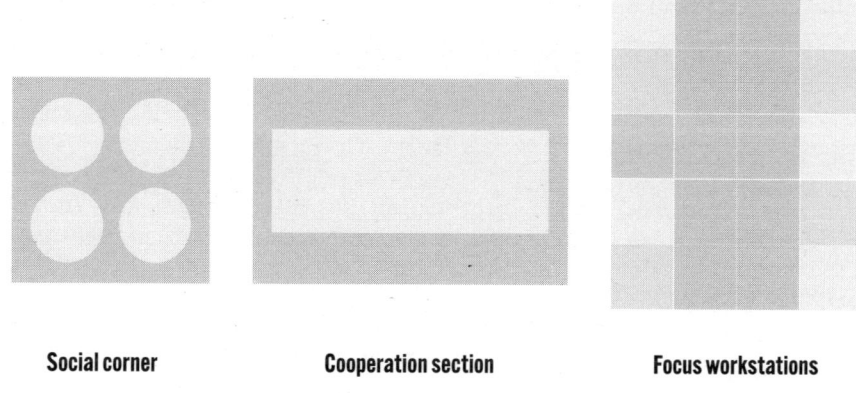

Social corner — Cooperation section — Focus workstations

workstations, quiet places where people work alone. This lets employees pick the spot that best suits their needs for the work they need to do.

Encourage Working from Home

Whether or not this works for you depends on your role. If it's an option, I recommend giving it a try. Most knowledge workers get more done at home than in the office jungle.

Block Off Quiet Time

Coordinating with your colleagues is as necessary as sharing weekend plans is fun. I couldn't imagine an office without either of these, but they can get annoying (for other people) if they happen all day. Someone's always talking in large spaces, making it more difficult for everyone else to get work done.

Quiet blocks are an effective solution. Agree, for instance, that you won't disturb one another between 10 a.m. and 12 p.m. No emails, no phone calls, and definitely no small talk unless the office is burning. You can still do all these things during the day, but only in the nonquiet blocks. People tell me how much they love this setup all the time.

You'll also find that it leads to better conversations and more quality time. Rather than listening to your colleague's story with half an ear as you work your way through your inbox, you'll be free to give them your full attention later on.

Offer Quiet Rooms

There have to be enough rooms where people can shut themselves off entirely. You'll find rooms like this in most offices, but never enough. You're expected to spend most of your time working in a room with others, but I believe it should be the other way around. Employers should encourage everyone to retreat to a quiet room for at least thirty minutes a day.

Invest in Sound-Absorbing Walls

Have you ever had a too-loud conversation with someone sitting at the same table? Chances are you were in a noisy room. The noisier our surroundings, the louder we speak, even if what we're talking about doesn't warrant it. This is known as the *Lombard reflex*.[9] It's like a vicious circle of noise where we keep getting louder to drown out other sounds. The circle's all too common when several people work in the same open space.

Modern technology to the rescue: you can counteract excess noise with sound-absorbing materials. You'll have to invest some money, sure, but you'll earn it all back by increasing productivity and reducing sick days.

For the record, I don't want you to become an asocial robot allergic to small talk with your colleagues. All I'm saying is that you should create an environment where you don't have to struggle just to be able to do your work. Remove the factors that make work difficult, and you'll find everything runs much more smoothly. As a nice bonus, you'll be a lot less annoyed by your colleagues, creating a much more chill work environment. When we're given the space to focus, we're 57 percent more effective when working with others, 42 percent more sociable, 31 percent more innovative, and 31 percent happier with our jobs.[10]

PRACTICAL TIPS FOR A MORE PRODUCTIVE OPEN-PLAN WORK ENVIRONMENT

Tip 1: Talk About It
- ✓ I can guarantee you're not the only one who isn't happy with your open office. Bring it up in a team meeting. See what you can agree on together. Introduce quiet blocks, for example, or propose that everyone switch off notifications.

Tip 2: Explore Your Own Way of Working
- ✓ As I mentioned before, there's a lot we can do ourselves to limit how much others distract us. Analyze how well you've mastered the other concentration leaks, especially emptying your mind and filling the void.

Tip 3: Buy Noise-Canceling Headphones
- ✓ These headphones neutralize ambient noise. Even if you don't use them to listen to music, they'll silence everything around you. Bonus point: wearing headphones lets your colleagues know that you're hard at work and not to be disturbed.

PART TWO

DEEP ATTENTION, CREATIVITY, AND TAKING CONTROL WHEN YOU CAN

THE CREATIVITY PARADOX

Why Defocusing Is Important for Gaining New Insights

Not so long ago, I was meandering around the supermarket when someone a few feet away started excitedly waving at me as if we hadn't seen each other in years. Embarrassingly, I had no idea who she was.

As she approached, I realized I did know her: we'd worked together for a few years and I should've known her name, but it just wasn't coming to me.

"Hi, Mark—how are you?" she asked when we were close enough to talk. Things were getting uncomfortable now; no matter how hard I tried, her name was stuck on the tip of my tongue. Despite my desperate efforts to figure out her name while we chit-chatted, I had no luck. The harder I tried to retrieve her name, the more my mind struggled. One embarrassing conversation and a slightly awkward goodbye later, she went about her day. I unlocked my bike and *bam!* Her name suddenly sprang to mind: Mary, I realized just a moment too late.* Sound familiar?

Why is it that when you consciously try to dig into your memory, the information you're looking for eludes you, only to suddenly appear when you call off the search?

Here's another common scenario: You're working on a complex issue—a real head-scratcher—but you just can't seem to find a solution. No matter how hard you rack your brain, you're not making any progress. Then, suddenly and unpredictably, the solution comes to mind. In the shower, during a walk, just before bed . . . but rarely when you need it. Why does this happen?

THE POWER OF THE SUBCONSCIOUS MIND

The information you're looking for (a name, a fact, a solution) is stored in your long-term memory. You're not aware of everything you know because all this information lurks below the surface. That's to our advantage: if we were aware of everything we knew, the abundance of internal stimuli would make us go mad. You wouldn't even be able to read this sentence. Too much baggage.

Over the course of history, a handful of people have had this awareness. The most famous example is a man named Solomon Shereshevsky, a twentieth-century Russian journalist. He never took notes during any of the meetings he attended, but when people asked him whether he was paying attention he could recite

---

* Mary, if you're reading this: Sorry!

conversations he'd heard two weeks ago, verbatim. He was such an oddity that it didn't take long for word about his remarkable gift to spread. Scientists lined up to study him.

They studied him for more than thirty years (voluntarily, for the record). Principal researchers concluded that Shereshevsky had "the perfect memory"; he was incapable of forgetting anything and was literally aware of all his knowledge.[1] This may sound like a great party trick, but it also had a major downside. Whenever Shereshevsky read the word "bike," for example, every bike he'd ever seen would flash before his eyes. As a result, his text comprehension was often rather poor.

Luckily, for most of us the bulk of our knowledge sits under the surface. It works as a filter of sorts, making it easier to focus on what we're doing. The practical challenge is that, because our knowledge is stored under the surface, we sometimes have to deliberately hunt down information.

When we dig for information, we usually focus our attention on the one thing we're looking for. You could compare it to a razor-thin laser. It can be a great tool, but it's not so handy when you're looking for your keys in a dark room. The greater your effort, the finer the beam, limiting your search area and reducing your chances of success.

This is exactly what happens when we feverishly try to remember a name. The more we look for it, the less likely we are to find it. In this case, focusing is actually counterproductive.

To allow names to resurface we have to defocus. We don't need a powerful laser; what we need is a lamp capable of lighting up the entire room. It'll make the search a whole lot easier. To defocus, we have to stop deliberately looking for specific information and go do something else. This passes the name search on to the subconscious mind, which is literally two hundred thousand times larger and therefore more powerful than our conscious focus, making it a lot easier to find information. That's why you don't remember the name of the person you just spent fifteen minutes chatting with until you're driving home in your car.

LESS FOCUS MEANS MORE CREATIVITY

Coming up with new ideas works in a similar way. Here too, defocusing works better than focusing. The area of the brain involved in generating new ideas is the frontopolar cortex.[2] This area becomes active when we defocus, and less active when we focus. Which makes sense: When we want to get something done, we don't want to wander off in all directions. It's better to head straight for the goal.

The first time I noticed the power of defocusing was when we hired an art director. We had often worked with freelance designers before, but this was the first time someone became part of our team. We immediately clicked and her portfolio was beautiful. But after the first few days our enthusiasm turned into doubt. She went on three walks a day and often sat staring out the window. And yet she created the most stunning designs and needed far less time than the external agencies we had worked with before. We didn't understand it until we dove into the science.

Creativity can't always be measured in hours. That's because part of the creative process happens in the subconscious mind, which is most active when you're not focusing on it.

Coming up with something new isn't something you can do efficiently from nine to five without any distractions. It's things like daydreaming, doing simple tasks, or going for a walk that actually support the creative process. To people who want or need to be productive, this might look as if creatives aren't taking their work seriously or aren't working hard. But nothing could be further from the truth. To reach creative insights, we sometimes have to stop being productive.

THE DIFFERENCE BETWEEN OPEN AND TARGETED ATTENTION

Another term for focus is "targeted attention," and another term for creativity is "open attention." These are terms we discussed earlier, and they go beyond just pressing the gas pedal or recharging. Open attention helps us find answers more easily, while targeted attention helps us get things done.

We need both types of attention. If we have only open attention, we don't get anything done. If we have only targeted attention, we're less creative and find it harder to solve problems. The key is to consciously switch between the two.

TWO TYPES OF ATTENTION[3]

OPEN ATTENTION	TARGETED ATTENTION
Defocusing	Focusing
Coming up with ideas	Implementing ideas
Thinking	Doing
Subconscious mind	Conscious mind
Recharging	Full speed ahead
Long blocks	Short blocks
Not absorbing new information	Absorbing new information
Time pressure inhibits open attention/creativity	Time pressure enhances attention/creativity

The writing process of the book you're reading now was a constant back-and-forth between the two types of attention: reading research (targeted attention), coming up with ideas and connecting different findings (open attention), and then turning those ideas into the text you're reading now (targeted attention again). I've found that the more I separate these phases, the easier writing becomes. You shouldn't try to paint a wall while you're still building it.

This need for a moment of nonproductivity during creative work is what I call the *creativity paradox*. When we operate in targeted attention all the time, productivity starts to drop, and it becomes harder to arrive at new creative insights.

The more creative the task or project, the more open attention you need. By consciously switching between open and targeted attention, you can steer both your creativity and productivity.

Understanding how the creativity paradox works gives us more control over our brains. It helps us tap into creativity when we need it most, making it easier to solve problems. Or, as the painter Chuck Close once said, "Inspiration is for amateurs." Just as there are conditions that help us focus better, there are also conditions that make it easier to be creative. And funnily enough, those two are exact opposites.

THE DIFFERENCE BETWEEN DISTRACTION AND OPEN ATTENTION

When I'm stuck on a difficult task, I sometimes find myself hoping an email will come in, just for a quick escape. If there's still nothing after refreshing my inbox a couple of times, I often read an article instead. You might think this helps creativity, since I'm no longer actively working on the task and my subconscious should now take over. But that's not how the brain works.

Taking in new information still counts as targeted attention, not open attention. And because we're filling our minds with even more input, there's no space left to really reflect on what we've already taken in.

Getting stuck on a task is a sign that our targeted attention is depleted. The best thing we can do at that point is to stop taking in new information. By doing so, we give the brain space to organize what's already there, clear things up, and start making connections.

What really helps is doing something simple that requires little targeted attention. New and unconventional ideas are easily dismissed by logic. The problem is that our logical reasoning is so well-developed that we do this almost automatically. By keeping our thinking brains busy with a simple task, we give our creativity the space to run free.[4]

For years, Albert Einstein worked as a clerk at a patent office, a job many considered far below his intellectual level. However, maybe he achieved his great insights not despite that job, but because of it.

CREATIVE MANAGERS

We sometimes have a tendency to glorify targeted attention. Getting as much done as possible, ticking off boxes on to-dos. Feels productive. But the price we pay is reduced creativity.

> The more clear-cut your tasks are, the more direct the relationship between input and output, and the more you rely on targeted attention. The less clear that relationship is, the more you depend on open attention.

Consider the commercial painter. It's pretty straightforward to measure how productive he's been. But now imagine he expands his business and has ten people doing the painting for him. He's mostly focused on managing the team and running the company. Suddenly, the input/output ratio becomes a lot fuzzier. When can you say you've been productive? Is it when you've cleared thirty emails, or just that one really important one? There's no simple answer to that.

As a manager, your job is more about solving problems, figuring out what needs to happen, setting direction, and coming up with new plans. In other words: creativity. Which means a greater need for open attention.

When you're just starting out at a company, your tasks are usually clearly defined by your manager: prepare this presentation, write that report, and so on. But as you gain experience, expectations shift. You're expected to figure out more on your own. Chances are, you'll also be managing people. The question becomes, Who comes up with the best solutions? Who has the smartest approach? And that requires giving open attention enough room to do its job.

Big corporations often focus on efficiency, trying to do more of the same. The emphasis is typically on targeted attention, like measurable key performance indicators (KPIs). But even there, the balance between different types of attention is crucial.

Maybe we can take a cue from start-ups, where chaos is often the norm. At Google, employees get one day a week to work on whatever they want. They call it "innovation time off," which is basically innovation through open attention.

You've probably heard the saying "work on your business, not in your business." It took me a while to understand what that really means. But a business contact once explained it clearly. "When you work in your business, you're mainly busy with tasks. That leaves little space to think about your business. The strategy. The direction. Ideally, you grow to the point where your own tasks are taken over, so you can focus more on the strategy." He's rarely at the office anymore. His team has taken over all operational work. He spends his time on the strategy of his company and knows he needs a lot of open attention for that. "It sounds like doing nothing," he said, "but it's one of the most important parts of the business."

CREATIVITY AND DISSATISFACTION

There's another element to this: the more we rely on creativity, the greater the chance we go home unsatisfied. That's because the whole creative process takes place beneath the surface, turning progress into a rather abstract notion and making it hard to track.

The same happens when I'm writing. I loved working on this book, but there were days when I got absolutely nothing done. No new ideas. Fragmented sentences. Nothing but a blank sheet of paper staring back at me. Very frustrating.

I eventually realized this didn't mean there was nothing happening below the surface. Oftentimes, tons of ideas arose in the days following these nothing days, giving me enough content to fill tons of pages. It might feel as though I came up with those words on the spot, but since most of the work actually took place below the surface, you'd have a hard time quantifying how much time it actually required.

It takes courage to make space for creativity by lying around doing nothing, and it can feel unnatural. As I said before, most of us feel the need to work hard to experience a certain degree of satisfaction, and I'm no exception. The challenge lies in finding satisfaction without necessarily doing anything.

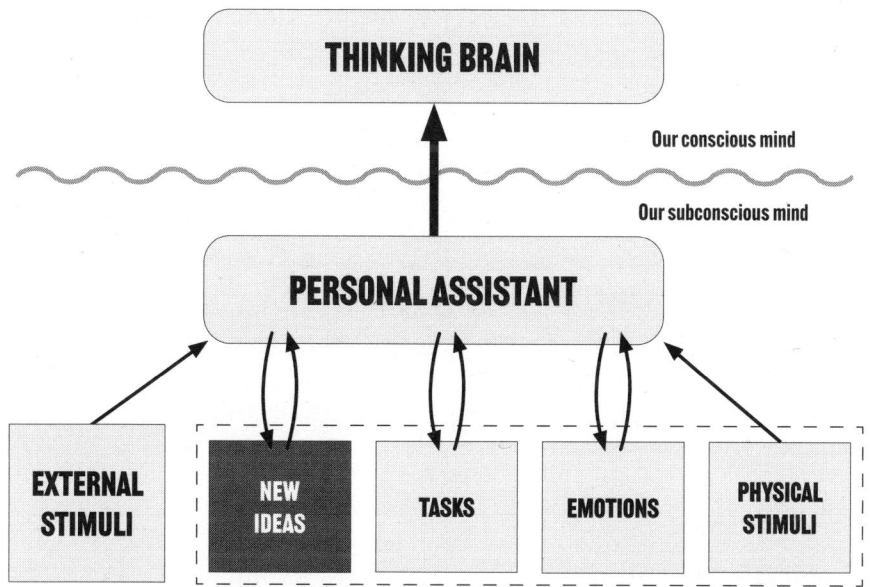

New insights and ideas take form in our subconscious minds, which by definition means that we're not aware of this process. We suddenly experience new ideas, unaware of the long process that preceded them.

STOP THINKING

Since I became aware of the difference between open and targeted attention, I've started making deliberate use of the two. Once I get stuck, there's no point in pushing harder on the gas. In fact, you're better off dialing down the intensity when you're stuck. Having a hard time remembering a name? Stop looking. Struggling with a problem? Go do something else. Not only is this more relaxing, it's also much more effective.

HELP, MY BOSS IS KILLING MY FOCUS

To What Extent Is Focus a Choice? (Part 1)

We're not alone at work. Colleagues are prone to throw a wrench in the works when it comes to your focus, in addition to making a lot of noise. Your boss is no different. Is your manager one of those people who demands that you reply within twenty minutes? They're out there, I know. Or does your director like to ambush you with new projects to be finished by, you know, right now? Corporate culture has a major influence on how we work. It's a huge factor in how much stress we suffer and how many people drop out of the race.

A knowledge worker without focus is like a painter without paint. Just as a painting company should equip their painters with quality paint and brushes, it's important for knowledge-intensive organizations to create an environment where their employees can focus. Focus should be facilitated. It's the number one way to boost productivity and reduce stress and sickness.

LEAD BY DISTRACTION

Let me start this by saying: managers are great. They chart our course, contribute resources to help us do our work, and the good ones keep the herd together. However, not all managers spend their Sunday afternoons studying *How Your Brain Works for Dummies*. Despite good intentions and efforts, some make it even more difficult to tick off tasks from your to-do list. Here are some of the most common managerial sore points:

1. A Tendency to Stack

Managers are often great at developing and launching new initiatives, but their most important duty should be deciding which projects not to work on for the time being. In the words of bestselling author Frans van Loef, OFFLOAD. Constantly setting new projects in motion without first clearing the clutter is counterproductive and leads to unhealthy workloads. As Van Loef points out, "Managers are often insufficiently aware of the fact that much more goes into implementing projects than into devising and launching them."[1] Hitting pause on certain projects immediately creates free space, reduces workloads, and allows more focus. "Stacking isn't the craziest tendency to have: most people don't really know how much capacity their organization has. A good first step is always to identify what everyone is working on. Meeting calendars and minutes provide more than enough information to come up with a comprehensive overview. Based on the organization's top priorities, divide the activities into three groups: go, time-out, and stop."

It's often easy to answer the question "Is this a good project?" with a hearty "Yes!" As a result, great projects pile up, which only hurts productivity and leads to unhealthy workloads. A better question to ask is this: "Which of these projects is most important?" It's the manager's job to determine what should not be done and prioritize the most meaningful projects. The biggest mistake a manager can make is to say, "All these projects have to be done, preferably by now. Good luck!"

If your manager doesn't tell you which projects to pick up and which to park, it's up to you to remind them. Try putting it as clearly as you can: "If you want me to do Y, I won't have time to work on project X. Which of the two is more important?"

Simplicity is everything. The more you manage to simplify, the more everyone can focus. Set a top priority for each quarter, along with no more than five other targets. If a project doesn't fit that list, get rid of it. Don't do it. If it's that brilliant, park it and return to it at some point in the future.

I regularly ask myself what I won't be doing in the next three months. There's always plenty of ideas and enthusiasm, but every project comes at a cost, whether it's time, money, or attention we can't devote to another project. This is also known as opportunity cost. As the lifestyle guru Tim Ferriss rightly says, "What you do is more important than how you do it." What all fast-growing companies have in common is a singular focus on one top priority.[2]

2. Expecting Immediate Responses

Some managers expect their team members to answer emails minutes after they're received. However, this unspoken agreement has a massive price tag.

It's immensely taxing for the brain to scan incoming messages throughout the day. If you expect your employees to respond to emails immediately, you should also expect them to take more time and make more mistakes in their other tasks. It's unrealistic to expect people to respond to messages quickly and remain fully focused at the same time. It's one or the other.

In my opinion, it's the manager's job to draw up a system and make expectations clear. Something along the lines of, Messages received on channel X must be answered within thirty minutes; for all other messages you have twenty-four hours. It's also up to managers to enforce the policy. Leading by example is always a good idea.

When managers don't clarify expectations, people tend to cut their own work short to respond to the boss's email as a matter of courtesy or hierarchy. They'll be quick to respond, but slow to finish their tasks.

3. Tolerating Frequent Interruptions

Continuing from my previous point, I believe organizations should give their employees the opportunity to spend at least one hour on their tasks without being disturbed. The more complex the work, the more time they should get.

Managers have to be proactive about focus hours, especially

if employees also have to respond to questions from customers or coworkers. No one wants business to grind to a halt during someone's focus hour, which means you need to decide who answers the phone when, who responds to time-sensitive emails, etc.

It's important that respect for the hour is ingrained in company culture: focus hours are sacred, and should be disregarded only when something is on fire. Or, as one of our clients did: "I gave everyone a squirt gun so they could shoot water at each other whenever they were disturbed during a focus hour." There was a steep learning curve.

4. Micromanaging

It's often thought that excessive workload is the main culprit behind employee absenteeism, but research conducted by TNO found that a lack of autonomy, or loss of control over one's own working style, has an even greater impact. In fact, it's to blame for 44 percent of all work-related sickness.[3] Because lack of autonomy is an important stress factor, it also indirectly affects our concentration.

The more control people are given over their own schedules, calendars, and tasks, the happier they'll be at work. Even giving people a simple choice works like a charm: "Do you want to work on Project A first, or would you prefer starting with Project B?"

5. Encouraging Long Hours

Hours worked is an easy metric for productivity; at least, it was when we all still worked in factories. As noted earlier, there's a negative correlation between the number of hours you spend behind a desk and your productivity. Today, it's the manager's job to make sure people leave the office. Go home. Recharge.

Don't get me wrong; I'm a big advocate of hard work. Of putting your pedal to the metal and achieving your most ambitious goals. But first, ask yourself this: What's the best strategy to get there? The way I see it, working ten hours a day only to go home and keep polishing off work-related emails isn't the way to go.

We have to get rid of the idea that it's cool to work long hours. It isn't. Long hours mean you're not in control. All too often we still equate being busy with being productive, but the opposite is often too true.

Since most people are trained to keep on working, simply saying they don't have to work long hours won't cut it. Implementing stopping cues is a lot more effective, and there are all kinds of ways to do so. One of my favorite examples comes from a design studio in Amsterdam. Their office is gorgeous, and clever to boot. If you look closely, you'll notice all the desks are connected to cables reaching up to the ceiling. It's very easy to miss . . . until the clock strikes six and all desks are automatically hoisted upward. It doesn't matter if you were sending the most important email in the world; after 6 p.m., work is off the table. (And the table is off the work floor.)

Something else to consider. Don't you think it's a bit too coincidental that everyone magically starts to tire at 5 p.m.? When you're exhausted, just go home. Continuing will only hurt your productivity. In many cases, embracing this idea will require organizations to totally transform their work cultures. Managers shouldn't count hours worked, but rather look at results.

Measuring productivity based on how long people spend at the office should be a thing of the past.

6. A Quick After-Hours Email

Now that we're connected 24/7 on our smartphones, we're gradually working more and more. We're always poised and ready to answer a message or two from our colleagues, no matter when they arrive. With good intentions, of course, we want to help others get their work done. Besides, urgent matters have to be dealt with eventually, even on your days off . . . right?

Not quite. It isn't healthy to regularly handle messages in your spare time or when you're on vacation. Resist the urge. It means your brain is constantly switched on and gets little time to recover.

In our company, we have a strict policy: no sending work-related emails or messages when the workday is over. The way I see it, it's up to managers to regularly make sure everyone understands why it's so important to switch off, and to integrate the practice into company culture.

An agreement not to contact one another after working hours is all well and good, but there are other ways, too. Mercedes-Benz, for example, set up its email servers to automatically delete messages sent to people on vacation. The vacationer will never know.

A SPECIAL NOTE FOR MANAGERS

DON'T OVEREMPHASIZE PRODUCTIVITY

Managers often tend to focus on results and productivity. Targets have to be met, of course, and productivity is easier to quantify than creativity. But focusing solely on productivity is too one-sided. Make sure to stimulate creativity, too.

It's easy. Get people to do nothing every once in a while. And I don't mean ordering groceries online; I mean nothing at all. A game of table tennis, perhaps. Or some good old-fashioned staring out the window. Create moments to drift off. Just like having dedicated focus workstations, setting up separate rooms for wandering thoughts works like a charm. People need a place to switch off.

TIPS FOR ENCOURAGING A PRODUCTIVE AND CREATIVE CULTURE

Here are a few practical suggestions for managers to encourage a productive *and* creative work culture:

Meetings: As Few and as Short as Possible

There's nothing wrong with the idea of coming together to make decisions, discuss ideas, or simply socialize for a while. It becomes a problem, though, when all we do is hop from one meeting to the next, leaving little time for actual work.

To understand the ideal length of meetings, please give another warm welcome to the Finnish school system, where classes last only forty-five minutes and school days are limited to five classes per day. It's a fairly unusual system compared with other Western countries, but as I mentioned before, it's led to fantastic results.

My advice? Do the same with meetings. If you really need more time for a particular topic, schedule several forty-five-minute blocks back-to-back. As long as there's at least ten minutes of break between each block, it shouldn't be a problem.

Leave If Possible

Meetings that don't have any added value for you are a waste of time. Elon Musk, the founder of Tesla and SpaceX, advised all his employees to simply leave unnecessary meetings. According to Musk, "Leaving a meeting isn't rude. What's rude is to force someone to stay and waste their time."[4]

Fight the Fragmentation

Scheduling meetings throughout the week has a fragmenting effect. One of my clients solved this by banning all meetings on Wednesdays, immediately transforming that day into an oasis of peace. It's also effective to schedule most meetings in the early morning and late afternoon.

Consider the Biorhythm of the Brain

Our brains are at their sharpest in the morning. It's a waste to schedule routine meetings during that time. Mornings are best used for meetings that require real thinking, brainstorming, or tough decision making. Keep in mind that this comes at the expense of other tasks the team could be doing during their prime hours. It's up to managers to make the most of their teams' golden hours. Sometimes that means scheduling an important meeting, other times it means protecting time for focused work. Late afternoons are better suited for simpler conversations and tasks that require less concentration.

ADDICTED TO DISTRACTIONS

To What Extent Is Focus a Choice? (Part 2)

You might recognize this: You just checked all your apps, you know there are no new emails or notifications, and yet you still can't resist checking your phone just one more time. Or you refresh your inbox every two seconds, silently hoping for new emails to arrive. I used to do this all the time. I was like a monkey feverishly pushing a button in the hope of getting a treat.

If you're the same, don't worry. You're not the only one. Multiple studies have shown that one in eight people is legitimately addicted to phones, and one in six of us is addicted to social media. Obviously I can't write a book about focus without bringing this up. The first question: Can we really work in an undisturbed, focused way if we want to check our phones or emails every other minute?

DISTRACTION BY DESIGN

It's not our fault that we can't resist our smartphones and inboxes; they were designed to be addictive. Developers and designers consciously set out to train us to use apps for as long as possible and to return to them whenever we can. The business model is simple: the more we use the apps, the more advertising space they sell, and the more their companies are worth. It works. In 2008 we spent an average of eighteen minutes a day on our phones. In 2018 we spent more than three hours a day on our devices.

All kinds of psychological tricks are used to keep us glued to our screens, starting with notifications. They're extremely difficult to ignore, which makes them the perfect tool for interrupting you and luring you to an app or website. Because they determine what we pay attention to, they're partly responsible for what our lives look like today.

Another clever technique developers use is removing so-called stopping cues. In the past, natural stopping cues were everywhere. You'd find your newspaper on the doorstep, read it, then go do something else when it was done. Digital newspapers, on the other hand, are endless. Every article ends with a link to a new one, trapping your interest and keeping you from moving on. The Pinterest app, for instance, was designed to always show you part of the next pin no matter what you do. Research proved this makes us more likely to keep scrolling. It's called endless scroll for a reason.

Email and social media apps were designed with the same principles as casino slot machines: you never know exactly when you'll get a reward. This is known as *variable reward*, and it's incredibly addictive. The first person to research it was an American psychologist named B. F. Skinner. Back in the 1950s, he conducted an experiment with pigeons. He put the pigeons in a cage with a lever. Every time a pigeon pressed the lever, it was given food. The system worked just fine: whenever a pigeon was hungry it pressed the lever. Skinner then modified the device to only occasionally give the pigeon food when it pressed the lever. In response, the pigeons went mad, constantly pressing the lever.

The constant urge to check your phone for new messages works in much the same way. You never know what you'll get. An amazing opportunity? Or a dangerous threat? Every time we receive a new message, dopamine is released in our brains, just like with the pigeons and their laboratory vending machine. Dopamine is a chemical that makes us feel happy, even if the message doesn't. All our brains care about is having something "new" to process. The same chemical is released when drug addicts do their substances of choice; the brain's initial response is the same whether you're taking a hit of meth or a hit of WhatsApp. The parallels between phone addiction and other addictions are clear. Phone addicts can't resist checking their phones for more likes or messages, drug addicts can't resist doing more drugs, and gambling addicts can't say no to another round on the slot machine. In all of these cases, the brain responds to the addictive stimulus in the exact same way.[1]

Dopamine hits are so addictive that you might feel restless without them. If you've ever left home without your phone, you'll know what it's like. The main reason we distract ourselves is because we're craving another hit of dopamine.

For the record, there's nothing wrong with dopamine. It's a fantastic neurotransmitter that motivates us to do new things and literally helps us to stay alive. The problem is that app developers take advantage of our innate need for dopamine to increase their revenues.

DON'T GET HIGH ON YOUR OWN SUPPLY

Fun fact: the brainiacs responsible for building our smartphones, tablets, and apps don't let their children use them. It seems the number one rule of drug dealing also applies to tech giants: don't get high on your own supply.[2] Steve Jobs confessed to *The New York Times* that his own children weren't allowed to have iPads.

FOCUS BITE

DIGITAL DETOX

Is a digital detox a good way to cut down on phone use? A German university studied this by dividing students into three groups. One group gave up their phones for seven days, the second group reduced their phone use by one hour per day, and the third group changed nothing. Surprisingly, cutting phone use by one hour a day had a better and longer-lasting effect than a full detox.

B. J. Fogg, a behavioral scientist at Stanford University, developed a method that can help reduce phone use. It's called Tiny Habits and has already been adopted by millions of people worldwide. The idea is to make the desired behavior small enough that it quickly becomes a habit. It also helps to link the new habit to something you already do.

The formula is this: After I [existing habit], I will [new tiny habit]. Example:

> After I get home, I will switch my phone to airplane mode. Or: After dinner, I'll put my phone in the kitchen drawer.
>
> Creating a new habit is personal. Keep it small and simple, and find what works for you.

THE DOPAMINE SPIRAL

Every time we get a hit from our phones, our brains crave more dopamine as a result; that's how we get addicted. Dopamine resembles sugar in that respect, once you take one bite of a sweet treat, you're probably going to take another. It works the same way in our minds: distraction creates distraction, in what I like to call the dopamine spiral.

Is unlocking your phone the first thing you do in the morning? Then that's when you activate your dopamine spiral, making it more difficult to focus for the rest of the day. Yep, that's how easy it is to fall behind 2–0 in the first five minutes of your day. Luckily, there's an easy solution: Don't take your phone to the bedroom. Buy an alarm clock instead!

There's another good reason to ban phones, tablets, and laptops from the bedroom: you'll probably have more sex if you do. Since the introduction of smartphones and tablets, couples' sex has been on the decline. During sex, our brains are flooded with dopamine that, if all goes well, should make us feel happy. But now we can get the same hit of dopamine by scrolling through Facebook . . . and that takes a lot less effort. Now, it's unlikely that our collective phone addiction will push humankind to the precipice of extinction, but it does clearly have an effect on relationships.

Out of bed and back to work: spending our breaks scrolling through social media makes it more challenging for our brains to focus afterward because they're still craving more dopamine. Avoiding social media altogether may not be a realistic option for everyone, but the longer we wait to open social apps, the easier it is to stay in the zone.

SMARTPHONES ARE ADULT PACIFIERS

Like any other addiction, frequently checking our phones is enjoyable in the short term, but has a negative impact on our well-being in the long term. We don't connect with others as much, don't have sex as often, don't sleep as well, and don't get as much done. There are even studies linking excessive phone use to depression. Despite the charming side effects, we still pick up our phones time and time again.

"Constantly spending time on your phone is essentially a sedative of sorts, a way to change your state of mind," Anne Sibon told me. She works as a psychologist and has specialized in treating all forms of addiction.

In recent years, she's seen the number of people seeking psychological help for their addictions skyrocket. "Now people automatically avoid uncomfortable feelings such as boredom or silence by grabbing for their phone; they've become less capable of coping with these feelings. As a result, we've become more vulnerable to the everyday setbacks that are usually part of life."

FIVE TIPS TO KICK THE HABIT WITHOUT KICKING YOUR PHONE OUT THE WINDOW

Just like leaving a toxic relationship, breaking up with your phone isn't easy. But it's worth it: taking the plunge will be a weight off your shoulders. Here are some tips that will help:

1. Keep Your Phone in a Drawer

We often keep our phones within reach so we can pick them up whenever we please. Putting more distance between you and your phone can help you resist temptation. When I come home, I often put my phone on the kitchen table. When I'm at work, I tend to leave it in my bottom drawer. I can still reach it when I need it, but making it slightly more difficult to reach means I won't be as likely to mindlessly pick it up. When my phone is right next to me, the temptation to take a peek every now and then is too strong.

2. Hide Your Guilty-Pleasure Apps

Another way to make phone usage more difficult for yourself is to hide your most addictive apps in a faraway folder instead of keeping them on your home screen. The more effort it takes to open them, the better. Moving your apps around every once in a while also works wonders: you won't be able to open them absentmindedly while you're doing something else.

3. No-Phone Dates

How many times have you seen a couple on a date who seem only to be looking at their phones? That's the last thing I want. When my girlfriend and I go out for dinner, only one of us takes a phone (for emergencies), puts it on ring, and leaves it in a bag. Going to dinner with friends? Put everyone's phones in a pile. The first one to look pays for all the drinks.

4. Digital Detox Days

When I go on vacation, I'll often go offline, too. A digital detox, as it were. It helps me let go of my emails, social media, news, messages, and so on. It's relatively easy to do this when you're on vacation, and the first time you give it a try I recommend trying to keep it up for three days. Pro tip: Tell your family and friends about your digital detox if you don't want them to organize a rescue operation when you don't respond for two days. I once made the rookie mistake of not doing this. Sorry, Mom.

5. Blocking Apps

If you're anything like me, you probably have your favorite apps you turn to for some well-earned relaxation. If so, have you ever noticed how easily five minutes morphs into twenty? Relying on willpower alone to keep yourself in check is a hard ask. Using blocking apps is a much better bet. These apps let you decide exactly how long you want to spend on your guilty-pleasure apps and sites. For example, you can choose to limit your time on Facebook to twenty minutes a day. When you hit the twenty-minute mark, Facebook is temporarily blocked. You can bypass the block, of course, but this takes some effort, making it an excellent speed bump. Personally, I use StayFocusd (Chrome), but WasteNoTime (Safari) and Cold Turkey Blocker (Windows) are good alternatives. iPhone users also have the option to limit their usage; look for the "Screen Time" section in Settings.

INBOX TO ZERO

Besides meetings, emails can also pull us out of our flow. On average, we check our inboxes seventy-four times a day, and I know people who reach that number per hour.[1] Email is a useful communication tool, but it often distracts us from what we actually planned to do. Writing that report or thinking about strategy? That can wait. First, let's deal with the emails.

Hardly anyone enjoys doing email, but at the same time, we can't and won't live without it.[2]

Getting an email is often just as disruptive as a colleague stopping by with a quick question.[3] After checking your inbox, your brain needs over a minute to recover and shift its focus to another task, like reading a document or having a meeting. Compare your inbox to the physical mail that drops through your mailbox. When we pick up the mail, we don't throw it back on the doormat after a quick look. We don't reseal an opened envelope once we've read it. And do you know anyone who walks to the mailbox seventy-four times a day to see if anything new has arrived?

Still, this is exactly how many people treat email. The result is fuller inboxes and less clarity. No surprise that just thinking about email stresses people out.

There are three types of emailers:

1. People whose inboxes are overflowing. Their strategy is simple: if it's really important, the sender will email again. We once had a man in our Inbox to Zero training with more than ninety thousand emails in his inbox. He was in the right place.
2. People who use a hundred folders and six different color codes. It's organized, yes, but it takes a big part of the workday to keep it that way.
3. People who use an effective system. They check their email a few times a day and stay completely up-to-date. Incoming messages: zero. No red notification bubble at the bottom of the screen.

I used to be in the first group. My inbox was a mess and a huge source of stress. Most of my replies started with "Sorry for the late response . . ." At first I thought that made me seem busy and important, until I realized I had missed out on some big opportunities because I had overlooked important emails.

Focus and a solid email system absolutely belong together. That's why, together with our team at Focus Academy, we developed a new Inbox to Zero training. It helps you reach inbox zero almost every day, with minimal time and effort. Being fully up-to-date with your email brings more calm, clarity, and control. More focus, less distraction. It's a relief.

The idea behind Inbox to Zero is simple: for every email that comes in, you immediately decide what action it requires. You don't have to do everything right away, but you organize it in a way that makes it clear what needs to happen.

INBOX TO ZERO IN THREE STEPS

The Inbox to Zero method consists of three steps to empty your inbox and keep it that way:

1. Set up a folder system
2. Use the decision model
3. Create ownership

Step One: Set Up a Folder System

Many people use their inboxes for everything: as a to-do list, archive, trash bin, and library all at once. But our brains struggle with unfinished tasks sitting in the inbox. That is why the goal of this method is to keep your inbox empty.

Put simply, every time we open our inboxes, our brains have to reassess each email. This takes a lot of mental energy. You can avoid that by moving emails into a dedicated folder. That small action signals to your brain that the task is being handled, allowing it to let go.

Creating folders makes it much easier to process and archive large volumes of email. One common trap is creating too many folders, which quickly becomes overwhelming and hard to manage. That is why we use a simple system of five main folders, plus one optional folder:

1. Action
Drag all emails here that still require something from you. The rule: only if the task takes more than two minutes.

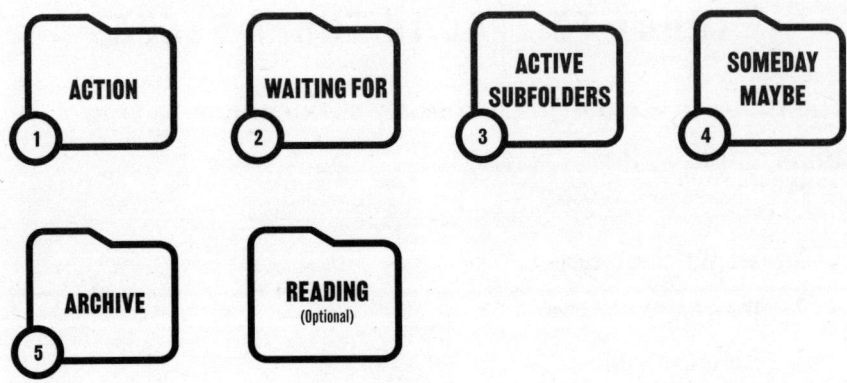

2. Waiting For

This is where you put emails when the next action is on someone else. It helps to keep all ongoing projects and delegated tasks in one place. This is your personal follow-up list. Check it regularly and follow up if needed.

3. Active Subfolders

This folder is for subfolders related to current projects you are actively working on.

4. Someday Maybe

Drag emails here with ideas or projects you do not have time for now but may want to explore in the future. Keeping them separate helps you stay focused on what matters today.

5. Archive

Archiving has one purpose: to find old emails when needed. To stop these messages from sitting in your inbox and silently asking for attention, move them here.

Optional: Reading

The optional folder "Reading" is a great place for things like meeting notes, reports, policy documents, or annual plans you still want to read. Block time in your calendar to go through these offline.

Step Two: Follow the Decision Model

Why is it so hard to quickly and effectively empty and process your inbox? A cluttered inbox often means we need to do something tricky: make decisions. Really, you're not the only one who struggles to figure out the right action for every email. Emails raise questions, and that's exactly why going through them can feel genuinely stressful.

The risk is that we deal only with the easy messages, giving us the illusion of being productive. Meanwhile, the more difficult emails, the ones that require thought, start to pile up.

A while ago, we had a participant in one of our trainings who was dealing with emails from early morning until late at night. It cost him a lot of time and energy. With his strong sense of responsibility, email was always a top priority for him. Strangely enough, his colleagues described him as someone who either didn't respond at all or always responded too late—much to his frustration.

What was going on? After a bit of digging, we found out he was also constantly answering phone calls and handling questions from colleagues. In other words, he was switching tasks all the time and never really got into the flow of focused email processing. The more complex messages, in particular, started to pile up, and he always felt that he was falling behind. That led to a constant sense of unease in his head, along with unnecessary stress.

He had lost control over his inbox. And he's not the only one. Many of us find handling complex emails unpleasant, often because we lack a clear overview, or because the sheer volume of work overwhelms us.

But in reality, it's rarely as bad or as complicated as it seems. It's usually our thoughts that make it feel difficult. It's just like back in school, when you kept postponing homework. Once you got started, it wasn't that bad, and you were done quickly.

To process your inbox more easily, it helps to follow a clear decision-making process. It gives you an instant overview and control over your workload.

Step Three: Create Ownership

Email often puts us in reactive mode. You don't have to think about what to do next; your inbox decides for you. The risk? You let the inbox dictate your focus, leaving planned tasks and projects untouched. The result: too little time, no clear overview, and that unsatisfied feeling at the end of the day. Fortunately, there's another way. You can take ownership of your tasks and responsibilities. When you act proactively, you take the lead, think ahead, and gain more influence over outcomes.

Using the decision model already gave you a head start. Now it's time to act on the tasks that take more than five minutes. While going through the model, you've placed these tasks in the first folder: "Action." Set aside, for example, one hour a day to deal with these. Depending on your role and how many emails you typically process, you might need more or less time. Someone in customer service usually has more email actions than someone in payroll, for instance.

Tasks that take longer than fifteen minutes have gone into

your to-do list. These require more time and attention and can't be squeezed in between other things. Tip: Block time in your calendar for these tasks. Planning them gives you more control over procrastination too. It's a win-win.

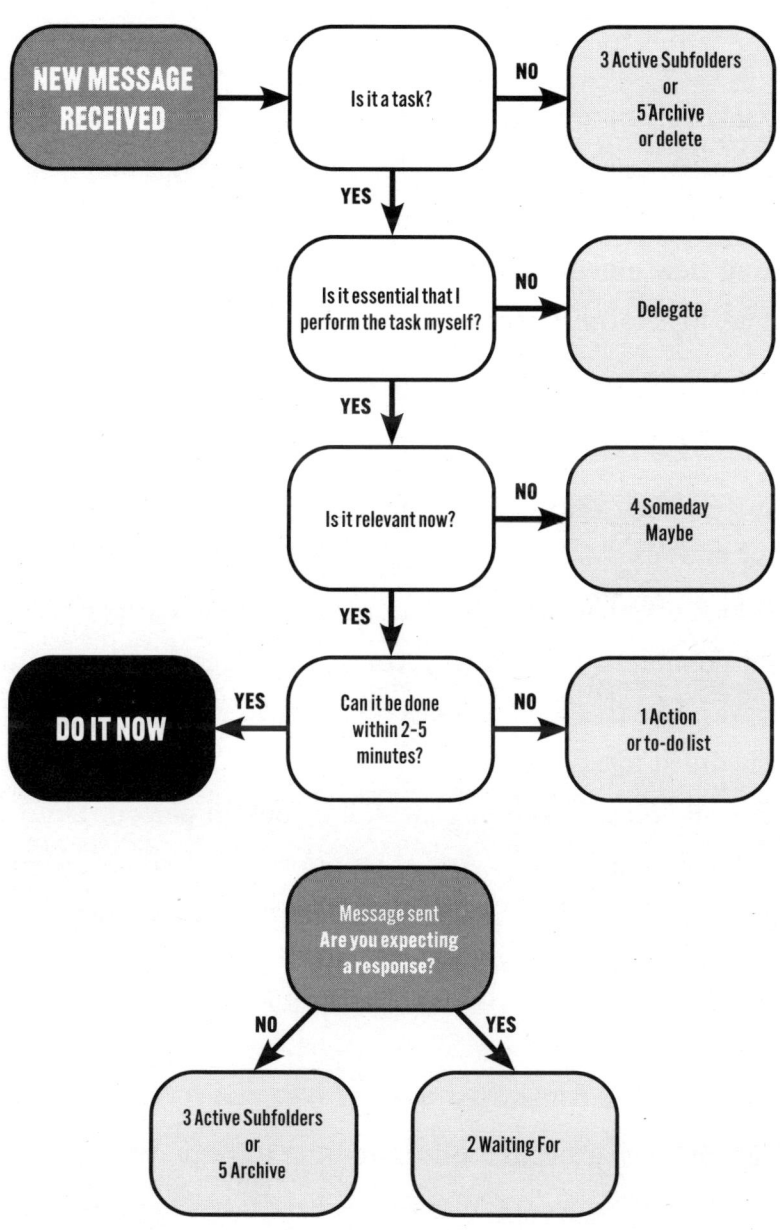

FIVE TIPS FOR AN EMPTY INBOX

Here are five more tips to help you and your colleagues keep that inbox empty:

Tip 1

Your email client is packed with features designed to make life easier: calendar, tasks, contacts, and so on. Handy? Absolutely. But it also makes it hard to look at your calendar without immediately spotting new emails. To avoid this temptation, it's better to use separate apps for different purposes.

Tip 2

There's no such thing as an urgent email. Feels good, right? No matter how urgent a message may seem, don't let it dictate your day. Block off a few email-free hours each day (or entire email-free days if possible) and don't let incoming messages pull your attention away. Use this time to focus on the tasks on your to-do list or on scheduled meetings.

If something is truly urgent, call or talk in person. Don't use email for urgent matters. And if emotions are involved, if you're sharing criticism, or if there's potential conflict, a conversation is almost always better than an email.

Tip 3

Got an email that needs a bit more time to respond to properly? Let the sender know you've received it and tell them when they can expect a reply. This saves you from getting a follow-up email asking, "Did you get my email?"

Tip 4

Use rules to sort quickly. This feature lets you automatically move incoming messages to specific folders. Perfect for things like newsletters.

Tip 5

Does your company not have an email etiquette yet? Propose creating one. A few clear agreements on how to use intraoffice email can save tons of time and prevent annoyance and misunderstandings. It also helps keep your inbox from overflowing. Here are a few suggestions:

KEEP IT SHORT AND TO THE POINT

Summarize your message so the recipient doesn't have to scroll endlessly. Before hitting send, read it again and cut anything unnecessary.

BE CLEAR

Structure your message with three parts: Context—Why are you sending this? Core message—What's the key point? Action—What do you need from whom, and by when? Clear and simple.

WRITE A CLEAR SUBJECT LINE

Let the subject line reflect exactly what the email is about. Stick to one topic per email. This keeps communication focused and makes it easier to find messages later.

BE SPECIFIC WITH CC AND BCC

One in five emails includes unnecessary cc recipients, people who don't need to act on or even know about the content.[4] We often do this to show others what we're working on. That's fine, but it clutters everyone's inbox. A better way is to share updates in the Monday team meeting.

USE EMAIL MORE DELIBERATELY

To: the person expected to take action
Cc: just for information, no action needed
Bcc: use only to hide recipient addresses

If you're emailing multiple people at once, clearly assign actions per person:

@Yara: Can you request the specs from client X?
Can you turn point Y into a presentation for client Z?

And finally: never hit "reply all."

FOCUS BITE

ARE WE HAPPIER WITHOUT EMAIL?

Yes, we are. That's what researcher Gloria Mark discovered in a live office study.

Participants wore heart monitors, and the researchers were given access to their computer activity. This way, they could track both stress levels and app usage. The group was split in two, and one half wasn't allowed to use email for twelve days. The results were clear: the more email people used, the more often they switched between applications, and the higher their heart rates.

So yes, we're happier without email. But we don't want to quit it. And we don't have to. These are our hacks:

Mark uses a tool called Adiós.ai to control when his emails arrive. He's set it up so that new emails get delivered only at fixed times during the day, for example, 11 a.m., 1 p.m., and 4 p.m. Like a virtual postman, all incoming mail is held back and delivered in one batch. Admittedly, he sometimes checks in between and fetches messages manually. But the more often he checks email or social media, the more it contributes to that empty, unsatisfied feeling at the end of the day.

Oscar doesn't keep his inbox open while he's working. To really get into deep work, he uses a double Pomodoro technique: uninterrupted fifty-minute work blocks followed by ten-minute breaks. After each fifty-minute block, he checks his email to see if anything needs his attention or if he can enjoy a proper break.

THE END

Thank you for reading this book! We hope you enjoyed it and that you have gained various insights to help you get a better grip on your focus. If you are enthusiastic, spread the word! You help us immensely by sharing our ideas with your friends and colleagues, and it's a good way for you to get even better at understanding the material.

If you're ready to put your new insights into practice, our free introductory course is a great place to start. In about fifteen minutes, you can identify your biggest concentration leaks at focusacademy.com/introduction.

If you have any questions, suggestions, or other things you'd like to share, please email info@focusacademy.com. The team at Focus Academy is eager to assist you.

Warm regards,

MARK & OSCAR

Acknowledgments

This book has been made possible by a whole group of people. First, we would like to thank our own team: Michelle Vonk, Sandra Hoekstra, Juun Hoyng, Irene Koot, Aalco van den Brink, Atilla Mohiddin, Robin Pera, Mirjam Pels, Eeske van Royen, Haiko Neidig, Vincent Heinink, Nina de Leeuw, Linda Abrams, Rosa-Lin Meijer, Jan Engelsman, and Marco Leijtens. The book has emerged and improved through many conversations with you all. Thank you!

Additionally, we would especially like to thank Renée Deurloo, Yvonne Brok, and Sladjana Labovic. The collaboration was a joy and without you, this book would never have come into existence.

Furthermore, there are countless others who have contributed thoughts during the writing process or who have provided feedback on earlier versions: thank you so incredibly much! The book has definitely improved because of this. Thank you all: Anne Sibon, Jochem Tigchelaar, Els Doornaar, Henk Tigchelaar, Svairin Sardjoe, Peter van Bergen, David Allen, Kathryn Allen, Tony Crabbe, Charlotte van 't Wout, Floris Wouterson, Yvonne Jordan, Jeroen de Boer, Manon ten Hove, Carlijn Tiekstra, Ellis

Gubbels, Pepijn Ouwerkerk, Marleen Oost, Arjan Broere, Ronald van Veen, Hanneke Goosen, Marco Bruining, Arno Rosendaal, Peter-Paul Oostveen, Dré van Melis, Miriam Hafkemeijer, Jacinta Nunes De Gouveia, Rianne Hamer, Annemarie Appelman, Tessa Rietveld, Roos Spanjer, Tim Jansen, Sandra Kroes-Ray, Maurik Dippel, Bram Speelman, Chris Olivers, Ed van Zwieten, Ilja Sligte, Raymon Middelbos, Artjanna Hulsmann-Harkhoe, Monique Bos-Wijers, Karin Poerstamper, Emily Franklin, Henriette van Balkom, Wim van den Berg, Anne-Marie Cuvelier, Tatiana van Lier, Hans Verbeeten, Loes Grooten, Janco Duvekot, Willem van der Ree, Frits Oukes, Lizette Kolmeijer, Ann-Lynn Hamelink, Carla van den Berg, Arno Rosendaal, Marcel Staring, Eveline Welling, Els Slob, Astrid van Leeuwen, Leontine van Roosmalen, Marijke Bouwhuis, Eveline Bollen, Renate Houtekamer, Arthur Korver, Petra Varenkamp, Menno van der Pijll, Tanja Slagter, Anke Geurtsen, Emeli Colen, Vera Sibon, Gerhard de Boer, Reinier van Dieren, Armando van der Bie, Ward Heeren, Larissa ten Veen, Eva Pavón Núñez, Peter de Bos, and Edo van Royen.

Glossary

15-MINUTE WORRYING SESSION

Technique you can use to relieve yourself of doubts or concerns. The steps are as follows: (1) write down your doubts or concerns, (2) for each item, decide what you should accept or what you can change, (3) do something that makes you feel good to get out of your current mood (e.g., get a cup of coffee).

25/5 RULE

Invented by Warren Buffett to make it easier to focus on goals, tasks, and projects. The idea is that you write down your twenty-five most important goals and circle the five most important ones. You have to ignore the other twenty goals to achieve the five most important ones.

ACETYLCHOLINE

Neurotransmitter that blocks distracting stimuli.

AMYGDALA

Area in our brain that plays an important role in emotions.

ATTENTION
See Focus.

ATTENTION RESIDUE
Our attention clings to whatever we were doing previously, which slows us down and causes us to make more mistakes. It's the main effect of the four concentration leaks.

BASAL GANGLIA CELLS
Brain cells involved in automatic behavior.

BUSYWORK
Habit of creating more work to stay busy. These tasks and projects often have little added value.

COCKTAIL PARTY EFFECT
Phenomenon that sees us suddenly shift our attention to another conversation when we hear our name mentioned at a party, for instance.

COGNITIVE DISTRIBUTION
Process of getting tasks, ideas, and emotions off your mind using a pen and paper, an app, email, or voice messages.

CONCENTRATION
See Focus.

CONCENTRATION LEAKS
Factors causing us to switch from one task to another, resulting in attention residue.

CREATIVITY PARADOX

Occasionally, we have to stop being productive in order to rest and foster creativity, so that we can be productive later on.

DECISION FATIGUE

Making decisions costs brainpower. The more decisions we make in a day, the harder it is to make the right one.

DEEP WORK

Term coined by Cal Newport to describe tasks that require more effort to perform but give the most satisfaction. *See* Shallow work.

DEFAULT MODE NETWORK (DMN)

Area in the brain activated when your mind wanders. When activated, it clears out your mind, so to speak.

DIGITAL DETOX DAYS

Days when you don't open your social media, WhatsApp, or e-mail to free yourself from digital distractions.

DOODLING

Making useless drawings, which can increase your focus by 29 percent.

DOPAMINE

Neurotransmitter released when we have new experiences. It makes us feel happy.

DOPAMINE SPIRAL

Every time we get a hit of dopamine, we need more of it and there's a risk of becoming addicted to the dopamine trigger (your phone, for example).

EXTERNAL DISTRACTORS

Things like email, our phones, and our colleagues.

EXTERNAL HARD DRIVE

Also known as the external brain. Place where you write down tasks, appointments, and ideas to get them off your mind. Simply put: pen and paper.

FILLING THE VOID

Because our brains think faster than we use them, they can easily wander. By making tasks more challenging, there is literally less room for internal and external distractors.

FLOW

Mental state in which we are fully consumed by what we're doing.

FOCUS

Ability to block distraction and bring yourself into a productive state of flow.

FRONTOPOLAR CORTEX

Area in the brain where we come up with new ideas; it becomes active when you defocus and let your mind wander.

GABA (GAMMA-AMINOBUTYRIC ACID) NEUROTRANSMITTERS

Chemicals that slow down the signals in your brain, making you vulnerable to distraction.

GETTING THINGS DONE (GTD) METHOD

Five steps formulated by David Allen to help you get more done and experience less stress. The five steps are (1) Capture, (2) Clarify, (3) Organize, (4) Reflect, (5) Engage.

GLUTAMATE-GLUTAMINE NEUROTRANSMITTERS (GLX)

Chemicals that stimulate the brain, helping you focus.

INATTENTIONAL BLINDNESS

When your attention is dedicated completely to one task, your perception diminishes.

INTERNAL DISTRACTORS

Includes ideas that suddenly spring to mind, tasks you realize you still have to do, and emotional thoughts (both positive and negative) that take your attention.

LOMBARD REFLEX

When we're having a conversation in a noisy room, we tend to speak louder, even though it's not strictly necessary.

LONG-TERM MEMORY

Umbrella term for our knowledge brain, creative brain, task brain, and emotional brain.

MIND SWEEP

Also called a brain dump. The act of emptying your head by writing down all your tasks and projects.

MIND WANDERING

Thinking of something other than what we're doing. Often an event in the past, but it can also be something in the future.

MULTITASKING

Performing multiple tasks at once without being aware of it; e.g., walking and talking.

NEUROTRANSMITTERS

Chemicals in our brains that transmit signals.

NORADRENALINE

Neurotransmitter that focuses our attention on what we're doing.

OHIO PRINCIPLE

Only Handle It Once. The purpose of this principle is to reduce the number of open loops. You can do this by (1) not starting tasks you know you won't be able to finish and (2) trying to close open loops as quickly as possible.

OPEN ATTENTION

You're processing information you've already absorbed, not taking in new information. Like daydreaming or spacing out—minimal effort required, and important for creativity.

OPEN LOOPS

Unfinished tasks or emotions stuck in our minds after a conversation, for instance.

OPPORTUNITY COST

Time, attention, and money spent on a certain project or task that can therefore not be spent on other tasks or projects.

PERSONAL ASSISTANT

Metaphor for focus. Also known as the gatekeeper. Your personal assistant determines which stimuli reach your conscious mind. Only 0.0003 percent of all stimuli we perceive are transmitted to our conscious minds.

POMODORO TECHNIQUE

Created by Francesco Cirillo in 1989, this technique revolves around focusing on a single task for twenty-five minutes before taking a five-minute break.

PREFRONTAL CORTEX

See Thinking brain.

RECOVERY TIME

Time we take to recover from switching tasks. (*See* Attention residue.) Our minimum recovery time is sixty-four seconds, but it can easily be as much as fifteen minutes.

SHALLOW WORK
Term coined by Cal Newport to describe tasks requiring little brainpower, which often give little satisfaction. Scrolling through LinkedIn, for example. *See* Deep work.

SHORT-TERM MEMORY
See Thinking brain.

STACKING (PROJECTS)
Refers to the tendency to start or assign new projects without completing or halting other projects first.

STOPPING CUES
Signals indicating something is finished, whether a simple cue such as finishing a physical newspaper, or a more constructed one such as electronics automatically shutting down at a scheduled time in order to force a stop.

SUPERIOR PREFRONTAL CORTEX
Area in the brain responsible for blocking distracting stimuli. The main neurotransmitter involved in this process is acetylcholine.

TARGETED ATTENTION
Effortful, conscious attention that helps you accomplish tasks.

TASK SWITCHING
Quickly switching between tasks requiring targeted attention (e.g., writing an email and having a conversation).

THINKING BRAIN

Area of our brains where we think, make decisions, and make plans. It's the central location of our IQs.

TRELLO

App that helps you track all your tasks and projects in an orderly fashion.

VARIABLE REWARD

When a certain action yields a reward in some cases and no reward in others, you'll never know what to expect. This is how slot machines work, and it's addictive for our brains.

VENTROLATERAL PREFRONTAL CORTEX (VLPFC)

Area in the brain responsible for blocking distracting thoughts.

VENTROMEDIAL PREFRONTAL CORTEX (VMPFC)

Area in the brain that determines how well you can regulate your emotions and how well you perform under pressure.

WORKING MEMORY

See Thinking brain.

ZENPEN.APP

The app to write away your stress (developed by Focus Academy).

Notes

1. Hilbert, M. "How Much Information Is There in the 'Information Society'?," *Significance* 9.4 (2012): 8–12.

INTRODUCTION

1. Stigchel, Van der, S. *Concentratie*. Maven Publishing, 2016.
2. Wilson, T. *Strangers to Ourselves: Discovering the Adaptive Unconscious*. Cambridge, MA: Belknap Press, 2004.
3. Wilson, *Strangers to Ourselves*.
4. Leroy, S. "Why Is It So Hard to Do My Work? The Challenge of Attention Residue When Switching Between Work Tasks," *Organizational Behavior and Human Decision Processes* 109.2 (2009): 168–81.
5. Gloria, M. *Multitasking in the Digital Age*. San Rafael, CA: Morgan & Claypool Publishers, 2015.
6. Gloria, *Multitasking in the Digital Age*.
7. Compernolle, T. *BrainChains: Discover Your Brain and Unleash Its Full Potential in a Hyperconnected Multitasking World*. Compublications, 2014.
8. Gloria, *Multitasking in the Digital Age*.
9. Rock, D. *Your Brain at Work: Strategies for Overcoming Distraction, Regaining Focus, and Working Smarter All Day Long*. New York: Harper Business, 2009.

FOCUS CHALLENGE: BOREDOM

1. Smallwood, J., and J. W. Schooler. "The Science of Mind Wandering: Empirically Navigating the Stream of Consciousness," *Annual Review of Psychology* 66.1 (2015): 487–518.
2. Killingsworth, M. A., and D. T. Gilbert. "A Wandering Mind Is an Unhappy Mind," *Science* 330.6006 (2010): 932.

3. Boyd, R. "Do People Only Use 10% of Their Brains?," *Scientific American*, February 7 (2008).
4. Tigchelaar, M. S. *Haal meer uit je hersenen*. Amsterdam: Prometheus, 2019.
5. Wong, L. *Essential Study Skills*. Boston: Cengage Learning, 2014.
6. Ashcraft, M. H., and G. A. Radvansky, G. A. *Cognition*. New York: Pearson, 2014.
7. Gwyer, P. G. "Applying the Yerkes-Dodson Law to Understanding Positive or Negative Emotions," *Clinical Psychologist*, September (2017).
8. Tigchelaar, M. S. *Lezen, weten en niet vergeten*. Houten: Unieboek | Het Spectrum, 2017.
9. Andrade, J. "What Does Doodling Do?," *Applied Cognitive Psychology* 24.1 (2009).
10. Tigchelaar, *Lezen, weten en niet vergeten*.
11. Compernolle, *BrainChains*.
12. Dunlosky, J., K. A. Rawson, E. J. March, M. J. Nathan, and D. T. Willingham. "Improving Students' Learning with Effective Learning Techniques: Promising Directions from Cognitive and Educational Psychology," *Psychological Science in the Public Interest* 14.1 (2013): 4–58.

FOCUS CHALLENGE: OVERSCHEDULING AND OVERCOMMITTING

1. Knight, R., and M. Grabowecky. "Prefrontal Cortex, Time and Consciousness," Knight Lab, Cognitive Neuroscience Research Lab, University of California at Berkeley (2000).
2. Bailey, C. *Hyperfocus: How to Manage Your Attention in a World of Distraction*. New York: Viking, 2018.
3. Mark, G., S. T. Iqbal, M. Czerwinski, P. Johns, and A. Sano. "Neurotics Can't Focus: An *in situ* Study of Online Multitasking in the Workplace," Conference Paper, May (2016).
4. Gloria, M., S. Iqbal, M. Czerwinski, and P. Johns. "Focused, Aroused, But So Distractible: A Temporal Perspective on Multitasking and Communications," CSCW 2015, New York: ACM Press.
5. Gloria, *Multitasking in the Digital Age*.

FOCUS CHALLENGE: A CLUTTERED MIND

1. Mack, A., and I. Rock. *Inattentional Blindness*. Cambridge, MA: MIT Press, 1998.

2. Levy, B. J., and A. D. Wagner. "Cognitive Control and Right Ventrolateral Prefrontal Cortex: Reflexive Reorienting, Motor Inhibition, and Action Updating," *The Year in Cognitive Neuroscience* 1224.1 (2004): 40–62.
3. Ophir, E., et al. "Cognitive Control in Media Multitaskers." *Proceedings of the National Academy of Sciences of the United States of America* 106.37 (2009): 15583–87.
4. Allen, D. *Getting Things Done: The Art of Stress-Free Productivity*. New York: Penguin Books, 2015.
5. Heylighen, F., and C. Vidal. "Getting Things Done: the Science Behind Stress-Free Productivity," *Long Range Planning* 41.6 (2008): 585–605.
6. Dijksterhuis, A. *Het slimme onbewuste*. Amsterdam: Prometheus, 2015.
7. Source: Mark Zuckerberg's Facebook page.
8. Saul, H. "Why Mark Zuckerberg Wears the Same Clothes to Work Everyday," *Independent*, January 26 (2016), www.independent.co.uk/news/people/why-mark-zuckerbergwearsthe-same-clothes-to-work-everyday-a6834161.html.
9. De Leth, R. *Oersterk in 6 weken*. Netherlands: De Leth Uitgevers, 2019.
10. Allen, *Getting Things Done*.

FOCUS CHALLENGE: BURNOUT

1. Manson, M. "How to Be More Productive by Working Less," March 12, (2017) https://markmanson.net.
2. Brown, S. B. R. E., H. A. Slagter, M. S. van Noorden, E. J. Giltay, N. J. A. Van der Wee, and S. Nieuwenhuis. "Effects of Clonidine and Scopolamine on Multiple Target Detection in Rapid Serial Visual Presentation," *Psychopharmacology* 233.2 (2016): 341–50.
3. Cirillo, F. *The Pomodoro Technique: The Acclaimed Time-Management System That Has Transformed How We Work*. New York: Crown Currency, 2018.
4. Pillay, S. *Tinker Dabble Doodle Try: Unlock the Power of the Unfocused Mind*. New York: Ballantine Books, 2017.
5. "The Relationship Between Hours Worked and Productivity," Crunch Mode, https://cs.stanford.edu/people/eroberts/cs201/projects/crunchmode/econ-hours-productivity.html.
6. https://www.legifrance.gouv.fr/jorf/id/JORFTEXT000032983213.
7. https://www.knack.be/magazine/hoe-denen-erin-slagen-nooit-overuren-te-maken.

8. Alderman, L. "In Sweden, an Experiment Turns Shorter Workdays into Bigger Gains," *New York Times*, May 20, (2016) www.nytimes.com/2016/05/21/business/international/in-sweden-an-experiment-turns-shorter-workdays-into-bigger-gains.html.
9. Berghmans, E. "Schaf de achturige werkdag af," *De Standaard*, October 20, (2016) www.standaard.be/cnt/dmf20161019_02528777.
10. Tigchelaar, *Haal meer uit je hersenen*.
11. Rosekind, Mark R., Kevin B. Gregory, Melissa M. Mallis, Summer L. Brandt, Brian Seal, and Debra Lerner. "The Cost of Poor Sleep: Workplace Productivity Loss and Associated Costs," *Journal of Occupational and Environmental Medicine* 25.1 (2010): 91–98.
12. Walker, M., et al. (2007). "The Human Emotional Brain Without Sleep—A Prefrontal Amygdala Disconnect," *Current Biology* 17.20 (2007): 22.
13. Tigchelaar, *Haal meer uit je hersenen*.
14. "Zes uur slaap per nacht kan even slecht zijn als helemaal geen slaap," *De Morgen*, March 8, 2016, www.demorgen.be/wetenschap/zes-uur-slaap-per-nacht-kanevenslecht-zijn-als-helemaal-geen-slaap-bed16623/?referer=.
15. Van Dongen, H. P., G. Maislin, J. M. Mullington, and D. F. Dinges. "The Cumulative Cost of Additional Wakefulness: Dose-Response Effects on Neurobehavioral Functions and Sleep Physiology from Chronic Sleep Restriction and Total Sleep Deprivation," *Sleep* 26.2 (2003): 11726.
16. Pilcher, J., D. R. Ginter, and B. Sadowsky. "Sleep Quality Versus Sleep Quantity: Relationships Between Sleep and Measures of Health, Well-Being and Sleepiness in College Students," *Journal of Psychosomatic Research* 42.6 (1997): 583–96.
17. Wouterson, F. *Superslapen*. Culemborg, Netherlands: AnderZ, 2018.
18. Wouterson, *Superslapen*.

FOCUS CHALLENGE: ALWAYS AVAILABLE

1. Fried, J., and D. H. Hansson. "Say No to Meetings! And 3 Other Ideas to Keep Your Workplace Happy and Healthy," Ideas.TED.com, October 10, (2018) https://ideas.ted.com/say-no-to-meetings-and-3-other-ideas-to-keep-your-workplace-happy-and-healthy.
2. Spira, J. B., and J. B. Feintuch. "The Cost of Not Paying Attention: How Interruptions Impact Knowledge Worker Productivity," New York: Basex (2005).

3. Begley, S. *Can't Just Stop: An Investigation of Compulsions.* New York: Simon & Schuster, 2017.

FOCUS CHALLENGE: TOO MUCH NOISE

1. Bernstein, E. S., and S. Turban. "The Impact of the 'Open' Workspace on Human Collaboration," *Philosophical Transactions of the Royal Society B* 373.1753 (2018), https://doi.org/10.1098/rstb.2017.0239.
2. Fried, Yitzhak, Samuel Melamed, and Haim A. Ben-David. "The Joint Effects of Noise, Job Complexity, and Gender on Employee Sickness Absence: An Exploratory Study Across 21 Organizations—The Cordis Study," *Journal of Occupational and Organizational Psychology* 75.2 (2002): 131–44.
3. Smith-Jackson, Tonya L., and Katherine W. Klein. "Open-Plan Offices: Task Performance and Mental Workload," *Journal of Environmental Psychology* 29.2 (2009): 279–89.
4. Compernolle, T. *The Open Office Is Naked.* Compublications, 2014.
5. Banbury, S., and D. C. Berry. "Disruption of Office-Related Tasks by Speech and Office Noise," *British Journal of Psychology* 89.3 (1998): 499–517.
6. Compernolle, *The Open Office Is Naked.*
7. Roberts, R. J., Jr., L. D. Hager, and C. Heron. "Prefrontal Cognitive Processes: Working Memory and Inhibition in the Antisaccade Task," *Journal of Experimental Psychology: General* 123 (1994): 374–93.
8. Brandhof, J. W. van den. *The Business Brain Book.* BrainWare, 2008.
9. Garnier, M., M. Dohen, H. Loevenbruck, and P. Welby. "The Lombard Effect: A Physiological Reflex or a Controlled Intelligibility Enhancement?," 7th International Seminar on Speech Production, December, Ubatuba, Brazil, 255–66 (2006).
10. Compernolle, *The Open Office Is Naked.*

THE CREATIVITY PARADOX

1. Luria, A. R. *The Mind of a Mnemonist: A Little Book About a Vast Memory.* Translated by Lynn Solotaroff. Cambridge, MA: Harvard University Press, 1968.
2. Green, A. E., and M. S. Cohen. "Frontopolar Activity and Connectivity Support Dynamic Conscious Augmentation of Creative State," *Human Brain Mapping* 36.3 (2015): 923–24.
3. Mark, et al., "Neurotics Can't Focus."

4. Mann, S., and R. Cadman. "Being Bored at Work Can Make Us More Creative," *ScienceDaily*, January 9 (2013).

HELP, MY BOSS IS KILLING MY FOCUS

1. Van Loef, F. *Stop met stapelen.* Culemborg, Netherlands: Van Duuren Management, 2014.
2. Harnish, V. *Mastering the Rockefeller Habits: What You Must Do to Increase the Value of Your Growing Firm.* New York: SelectBooks, 2002.
3. Wiezer, N., R. Schelvis, M. Van Zwieten, K. Kraan, M. Van der Klauw, I. Houtman, J. H. Kwantes, and M. B. Roozeboom. "Werkdruk," TNO (2012) https://www.tno.nl/media/1132/werkdruk_tno_rapport_r12_10877.pdf.
4. Loria, K., and J. Kanter. "These Are 8 Strict Workplace Rules Elon Musk Makes His Tesla Employees Follow," *Business Insider*, June 13, (2019) www.businessinsider.nl/elon-musk-productivity-tips-for-teslaemployees-2018-4/?international=true&r=US.

ADDICTED TO DISTRACTIONS

1. SWNS. "Technology Addicts Suffer Same Withdrawal Symptoms as Heroin Addicts, Therapist Finds," *New York Post*, February 17, (2025) https://nypost.com/2025/02/17/lifestyle/technology-addicts-suffer-same-withdrawal-symptoms-as-heroin-addicts-therapist-finds.
2. Baneke, I. "Verslaaft aan je smartphone," *Trouw*, April 27, (2017) www.trouw.nl/home/verslaafd-aan-je-smartphone~aa52a1ba/.

INBOX TO ZERO

1. Gloria, *Multitasking in the Digital Age.*
2. Eyal, N. *Hooked: How to Build Habit-Forming Products.* New York: Penguin Books, 2014.
3. Jackson, T., R. Dawson, and D. Wilson. "The Cost of Email Interruption," Journal of Systems and Information Technology 5.1 (2004).
4. Jackson, et al., "Cost of Email Interruption."

About the Authors

MARK TIGCHELAAR is a psychologist, bestselling author, and one of the leading experts on focus and attention. He is a highly sought-after keynote speaker at international conferences, where he translates neuroscience into practical tools to improve focus, performance, and well-being. You can book him directly via mark tigchelaar.com.

OSCAR DE BOS is the founder of Focus Academy, a training company that helps professionals master the science of productivity and focus. Together with his team, he develops practical tools ranging from workshops and keynotes to apps, videos, and books.